CAUGHT IN THE ACTS

Sermons For Lent
And Easter
Cycle A, First Lesson Texts

G. EDWARD WHETSTONE

CSS Publishing Company, Inc.
Lima, Ohio

CAUGHT IN THE ACTS

Copyright © 1995
CSS Publishing Company, Inc.
Lima, Ohio

All rights reserved. No part of this publication may be reproduced in any manner whatsoever without prior permission of the publisher, except in the case of brief quotations embodied in critical articles and reviews. Inquiries should be addressed to: Permissions, CSS Publishing Company, Inc., 517 South Main Street, P.O. Box 4503, Lima, Ohio 45802-4503.

Scripture quotations are from the *New Revised Standard Version of the Bible*, copyright 1989, by the Division of Christian Education of the National Council of the Churches of Christ in the USA. Used by permission.

Library of Congress Cataloging-in-Publication Data

Whetstone, G. Edward, 1945-
 Caught in the acts : sermons for the first lesson, Lent-Easter : Cycle A / G. Edward Whetstone.
     p.   cm.
   ISBN 0-7880-0443-3
   1. Lenten sermons. 2. Eastertide-Sermons. 3. Bible-Sermons. 4. Sermons, American. I. Title
   BV4277.W48   1995
   252'.62-dc20   95-13909
                                                                                CIP

This book is available in the following formats, listed by ISBN:
0-7880-0443-3 Book
0-7880-0444-1 IBM 3 1/2 computer disk
0-7880-0445-X IBM 3 1/2 book and disk package
0-7880-0446-8 Macintosh computer disk
0-7880-0447-6 Macintosh book and disk package
0-7880-0448-4 IBM 5 1/4 computer disk
0-7880-0449-2 IBM 5 1/4 book and disk package

PRINTED IN U.S.A.

to my loving families

my parents
George E. and Katherine Steck Whetstone

the parishes which nurtured me through childhood
and these beloved partners in ministry:
the Sharpsburg Parish and Salem, Catonsville in Maryland

Victoria,
Micah and Linsey

Table Of Contents

Foreword — 7

Ash Wednesday — 11
Now, Even Now ...
Joel 2:1-2, 12-17

Lent 1 — 17
Down A Garden Path
Genesis 2:15-17; 3:1-7

Lent 2 — 21
God Works Wanders
Genesis 12:1-4a

Lent 3 — 25
God's A Catcher
Exodus 17:1-7

Lent 4 — 31
In The Eyes Of God
1 Samuel 16:1-13

Lent 5 — 35
It Ain't Over 'Til It's Over
Ezekiel 37:1-14

Passion/Palm Sunday — 41
Our Champion Rides Into Battle
Isaiah 50:4-9a

Maundy Thursday — 47
A Cross For A Doorpost
Exodus 12:1-4 (5-10) 11-14

Good Friday   **51**
    A Day Like Two Thousand Years
    Isaiah 52:13—53:12

Easter Day   **61**
    All The World Is Waiting For The Sunrise
    Acts 10:34-43

Easter 2   **67**
    Caught In The Acts
    Acts 2:14a, 22-32

Easter 3   **73**
    Standing And Understanding With The Apostles
    Acts 2:14a, 36-41

Easter 4   **77**
    Not Independence, But Freedom
    Acts 2:42-47

Easter 5   **81**
    Our Defense In A Stone-littered World
    Acts 7:55-60

Easter 6   **87**
    Paring Down Our Pantheons
    Acts 17:22-31

Easter 7   **93**
    People With A Mission
    Acts 1:6-14

Ascension Of The Lord   **99**
    Sometimes Goodbye Is Hello
    Acts 1:1-11

Foreword

The seasons of Lent and Easter find us *Caught In The Acts* — caught in the acts of those who are both saints and sinners all at once, *simul justis et peccator*, as Luther said. The Old Testament lessons of Lent challenge us to examine ourselves, to repent, and to accept the forgiveness of our merciful God. The Easter lessons from Acts challenge us to celebrate our Lord's resurrection by living free and faithful as his saints, with examples such as Peter, Stephen and Paul.

There is a pattern through these sermons for each season, clearly identified in Easter but not specifically named in Lent.

The sermons for Lent 1 through Lent 5, though never referred to by name, move through the first seven of the Twelve Steps of Alcoholics Anonymous. Across the years I've learned much from the witness and example of some of my members, whose experience in various 12-step programs has given them a calm, a self-esteem, a graciousness, a spirituality and joy in life which I've much admired. Among others, I know I'm indebted to Ginny (now with the Church Triumphant), to Tom and Lynn, to Leslie, David and Donna.

The direction of the lessons through Lent seemed to naturally suggest the progress of the 12 steps. The first step, which concerns our need to admit that we are powerless by ourselves to manage our own lives, is addressed on Lent 1 through the story of Eden's garden and the foolishness of trying to serve as our own gods. The second step, the belief that God is able to guide us to stability and sanity, is conveyed on Lent 2 in the courage of Abram and Sarai to venture into an unknown but promised and promising future. The commitment to turn our wills and our lives over to God's care, the third step, is carried in the story of the Jews in the midst of all the unfamiliar challenges of the wilderness on Lent 3.

The lesson which describes God's choosing David as King on Lent 4 demonstrates confidence in the unconditional love of God through the fourth and fifth steps, which focus on our need to reflect upon our failings, to take inventory, to repent and to confess our sins. The sixth and seventh steps, seeking courage to have God remove our sins and make a new beginning, are dealt with in God's promise of new life for the valley of dry bones on Lent 5. The eleventh step (seeking a closer relationship with God, and praying for knowledge of his will and the power to follow it) along with the twelfth step (sharing our spiritual awakening with others) continues naturally throughout the Easter season and all of our preaching.

The theme of the Easter sermons is our celebration of the resurrection of our Lord through the gifts of the Spirit. The sermons for Easter 2 through Easter 7 each focus on one of the gifts of the Spirit as named by Isaiah: wisdom and understanding, counsel and might, knowledge and the fear of God, joy in his presence. This is explained in the sermon for Easter 2, and identified at the beginning of each Easter sermon. Saint Luke's story of the early Church in the Acts of the Apostles is an exciting and dynamic witness of the power of the resurrection. In hearing again these lessons this season we seek ourselves to be *Caught In The Acts* of the Apostles and their successors.

Sermons for the festival days all seek to retell, explore, and celebrate the most familiar and dramatic stories we know in less conventional forms and images. I suspect for most of us preachers, conveying the power of the gospel on the festivals may be the most demanding and exciting aspect of our preaching.

Like every preacher, I'm deeply indebted to the parishes where I've served. It's not just their feedback which has helped to shape my preaching, but their lives. It's being aware of their needs and joys and pains and dreams which has challenged me to express the gospel story in a way which is clearly pertinent to the routine and exceptional events of all of our lives. It's a challenge which I know I meet only inconsistently. And surely only then by God's grace.

I'm forever grateful to the congregations which I've been blessed to serve: my seven years with Mt. Zion in Locust Grove, Holy Trinity in Sharpsburg, and Salem at Baker's Crossroads, and these last 17 years with Salem in Catonsville, Maryland.

Through all the years of my ministry I've been blessed with a supportive family. My father, now retired, was my first preacher and I still sometimes hear him in my own voice as I preach. My mother was always active in the church and community in her own right, and most all my sensibilities derive from her. Faithful to their Lord and deeply committed themselves to his Church, my wife Vicky, son Micah and daughter Linsey have been understanding, patient and supportive in the preparation for this deadline. As they always are.

Special thanks is due to Vicky and to my good friend Linda Burns for the typing and proofreading of this manuscript, along with their helpful suggestions for its improvement.

I'm grateful to the publisher for the opportunity to share these sermons with you. If there is anything here which enriches your pleasure in the gospel, or which you might find useful in your own proclaiming of the gospel, I'm thankful to him who is the source and author of every good and useful thought. By his grace, we are not only caught in the acts of being human, but we are caught in the mighty acts of God!

G. Edward Whetstone

Ash Wednesday
Joel 2:1-2, 12-17

Now, Even Now ...

I can imagine castles in the air and kingdoms under the sea. I can picture a phoenix rising from an ashy fire or elves riding crickets on the forest floor. I can imagine a thousand fanciful things better than I can imagine my own death.

I've always seen the world only through my own eyes, comprehended it with my own mind, loved it with my own heart. How can I conceive of the world without me in it? So I persist in my illusion that I will always be here. I struggle not only with a fear of death, but the fact that my death seems so unreal. I suspect that most of you are much like me.

In the midst of our illusory immortality, Ash Wednesday traces the warning right on my forehead and my soul, yours too: "Remember that you are dust and to dust you will return."

What if we were really to take this to heart and mind and accept the necessary reality of our own deaths, the brevity of our years? It's a reality which crisis or advancing age or powerful grief forces some to confront. Maybe some among us this night. Death, it's true, is not a distant stranger to all of us.

So if we really did accept that we will not live forever, how would it change things? What difference would it make? We hear of people, suddenly aware that they don't have long to live, saying that they intend to quarrel less, laugh more, more often stare into the night sky and stay in closer touch with their families and friends. Of course, for some, the reality of nearing death brings profound fear or despair.

What prevents us from living so keenly aware of the blessings, needs, possibilities, dangers and beauty of this day and each day? Actually, people have a lot of trouble holding on to the present moment.

Some people long for an imaginary past. They sigh for simpler times, for the good old days. They conjure up a happier time, in their own lifetime or even of sometime before their life. They wistfully recall when trolleys clacked up and down the avenue, when the whole family gathered around the radio. They think of special nights filled with the music of Glenn Miller or Rosemary Clooney or the Platters or the Beatles; it all depends on the wonderful yesterday that fills their senses. Even in the church, there are people who hunger for an age when hymns seemed sweeter, sermons more compelling, pews more full. They know there was a time when faith was less complicated, more solid. Some people want to live in an imaginary past. Do you?

Of course, some people are trying to live in the future. They're waiting to get another job, to get married, or for when the kids get older, or when they retire. They're holding out for the time when society straightens out all these stressful and dangerous ills which fill the news and keep them back. Maybe they're just always waiting for their next vacation, or even for the weekend. In church, they wait for all their doubts to be assuaged, for more people to come, for a new pastor or for the day when they'll really have time to study the Bible. Some people are so focused on the future they find it difficult to concentrate on the present. Do you?

Some people live in a world that never was and never will be. They daydream of what might have been. If only they'd been raised in a family that had more advantages. If only they had worked harder in school. If only they were prettier, or more athletic, or had more money. If only they were married to someone else, or if their children were more like some other children they know. Sometimes they drown in their daydreams of what might have been. Some people. You?

Living in the past or the future or fantasy: all prevent us from living in the present. Maybe that's not entirely unintentional. In the present there are so many ordinary things to do and do all over again. The present is full of hassles and tedium and disappointments and complications. It's certainly not that we don't need to remember the past and anticipate the future. Indeed memory and hope are key biblical themes. But it is memory for the real past — our personal past and the history of God and his people. And it's hope for a real future — our own and God's promises for the whole world. Even daydreaming has its place: diversion, wonder, exploration and play. But we dare not daydream too long, not so long that we lose our grasp on the present moment.

"Yet even now," begins our reading from Joel. "Even now, says the Lord, return to me with all your heart, with fasting, with weeping and with mourning." We are called to remember our past, the past we may wish to forget but need to remember. Remembering, we know we have not loved God with our whole hearts, nor have we loved our neighbors as ourselves. So we fall on our knees and repent and pray for forgiveness. "Now," our scriptures begin — our Lent begins — repent and return to the Lord. The reading from Paul continues the theme as the passage concludes, "Now is the acceptable time; behold, now is the day of salvation." "Now" indeed encompasses not only our past, but also our future. The present is bound with memory and hope.

Now is the moment we begin this holy time. What better season than this Lent, what better day than this Ash Wednesday, what better moment than this one to commit ourselves to reflect, to repent, to hope and to make a new beginning? God's grace lives best for us in this present moment.

The present, after all, is filled with more than frustration and stress. The present moment also holds opportunities to meet challenges, to conquer fears, to be healed of guilt and pain, to savor the rich blessings God gives us. All this is possible in the present moment.

Throughout this Lententide we'll focus on this commitment. We'll recognize what fools we are to seek to be the lords of our own lives, and we'll seek to let our living God reign over us.

We'll venture forward, letting God guide us into our yet unknown future. We'll admit that seeking new life in God's grace is not easy or comfortable, but that the rewards are incalculable. We'll learn to see ourselves not like the world sees us nor even as we may have once seen ourselves, but we'll seek to see ourselves in God's eyes as we really are — loved and valued beyond measure. In God's eyes we'll also begin to see the person who, by God's grace, we are already becoming. We will take heart that the resurrected Christ has come into our world and into our lives so we may find new life, even now.

There's little reinforcement in the world around us to set aside this season for such a holy and healing purpose. There will not be obvious signs of this season's presence where we work or shop. The air will remain chilly and the dark will come early and stay late. Yet in here our liturgy adopts some sobering shifts. Our hymns are often more plaintive. The "alleluia" is buried until Easter. You can mirror these changes in your own devotions. Use prayers of reflection and repentance and renewal. You can fashion your own reminders of your commitment on your desk or at the sink or your bedside. Then be ready to celebrate the joy of Easter, and the gift of new life and life eternal.

The ashen cross on our foreheads may not make it any easier to imagine our own deaths, but it is intended to press upon us its reality. To know the reality of one's own death is not for the Christian a morbid exercise. It saves us from the illusion that this life will go on forever. Aware of the brevity of our lives and our own necessary deaths, we can truly make the most of the time.

"*Now*," writes Joel, "return to the Lord with all your heart." "*Now*," Paul affirms, "is the acceptable time, *now* is the day of salvation." This is our holy *carpe diem*, a real "seize the day"!

You see, we wear more than one cross on our foreheads tonight. We don't only wear the ashes of our mortality. The second is the invisible but cherished and life-giving cross placed on our foreheads at baptism. "You have been sealed by the Holy Spirit and marked with the cross of Christ forever."

We don't live in the past, but we remember, repent and are reconciled. We don't live in the future, but we hope and know that

God is already working his salvation in us. We live in the present, and in this present we commit ourselves to a holy season of healing and grace. We have a beloved communion hymn which knows no tense but the present. In its stanzas there are no "were's" or "will be's." Just "now."

> *Now the silence, Now the peace, Now the empty hands uplifted;*
> *Now the kneeling, Now the plea, Now the Father's arms in welcome;*
> *Now the hearing, Now the pow'r, ... Now the heart forgiven leaping;*
> *Now the Spirit's visitation, Now the Son's epiphany,*
> *Now the Father's blessing.   Now. Now. Now.*
> (from "Now The Silence" by J. Vajda)

Lent 1
Genesis 2:15-17; 3:1-7

Down A Garden Path

Imagine being set in a lush garden with all kinds of flowers, plants and trees. There are lemon trees, fig trees, olive trees, date palms, oranges and apples. The Lord says, "You may freely eat of every tree in the garden, but of the tree of the knowledge of good and evil you shall not eat."

How hard could it be? All those trees, boughs lush with so many succulent and delicious choices. How could you get caught with your mouth full of the forbidden fruit! The subtle pressure of a smooth-talking snake doesn't seem sufficient to explain such audacity or stupidity.

Put us in a garden and perhaps we could handle it! Or how about a desert? Jesus is in a swirl of sand and sun, of Satan's remarkable and recurrent presence, of prowling beasts and the beat of angels' wings.

We might believe, foolishly, that set in a garden or a wilderness we could resist temptation. Give us a chance to try it in a space set apart from the routines of our daily lives — to mark the tree, to identify the enemy and gather grace to resist.

How much more difficult it is to sort it all out — what's faithful and what's not — in the complex web of routines and crises of our daily lives! Seldom do our temptations seem so specific, so frightening, so sudden or so foreign, as the temptations in the garden or the desert.

We find ourselves at the onset of Lent placed in no garden or in no wilderness. We've gotten up and made coffee, scanned the Sunday paper, fed the cat, dressed the children, checked the stove, locked the door and done a dozen simple things we've done so often we couldn't recall them all — just to be here. What does this world of ours, so familiar and commonplace, have to do with the extraordinary, larger-than-life stories of the garden and the desert? Everything. Though they have meanings greater and wider than our own personal application, they also have a profound meaning for each Christian's life.

Couldn't we resist the fruit of just one tree? It doesn't sound so bad. What if there had only been one rule in our elementary school? What if in our job training seminar there had been just one simple guideline? What if Moses had come down the mountain saying, "Everybody take heed to these tablets, though I don't know why there are two whole heavy tablets when there's just one commandment!"

Just one commandment! But what if that one commandment encompassed everything? What if it's a commandment like "You shall love the Lord your God with all your heart and mind and strength?" *That's* the meaning of the tree in the garden. They specifically wanted to seize power from God. They weren't satisfied with all they had been given. They wanted to be their own gods.

Jesus in the desert rejected the temptations to join with the Evil One in displacing God. "You shall only worship the Lord your God and you shall serve only him!" There is no god but God, Jesus declares. And there's no one poorer to try to take his place than ourselves!

So how foolish and dangerous it is that we seek to live our lives as though we had no need of God, as though we are our own gods. We want to live as though we can take care of ourselves, as if we could ignore God and his wiser purposes for our lives. Or we still invoke his name, but try to shape God and his love and power to what *we* want. We're ready to sacrifice, love our neighbor, work for peace and justice — but only on our own terms. We pray to change God, not to allow ourselves to be changed.

When we live this way, we severely jeopardize not only our ability to praise and serve God, but also the opportunity for him to work in us his blessing and our fulfillment. Our lives can drift and slide into chaos so easily that we may lose sight of our perils. It is so important, then, that we say at Lent's beginning and the beginning of each day that we ourselves are powerless to direct our lives in the way of peace and fulfillment!

It's not what we want to believe about ourselves. From our early years we are taught to achieve, to excel, to succeed. And the measures of success have always been clear: good grades, athletic skill, a pretty face, a successful career, a luxurious house. As the years have gone by, we've learned, often the hard way, that we are not in control. Our fears and doubts and insecurities have increased too. No one succeeds in everything. No one has it all. At least, not in the world's terms.

So this is our Lenten focus: to know that we are God's, and only through him will we succeed in having control over our affairs and our destinies. Then with Paul, we say, "When I am weak, then I am strong."

We struggle in this faith amid the most ordinary activities of our lives. If we assume our faith is just a church thing, or just something for the greatest crises of our lives, then what will prepare us for those thousand temptations that steal over us in the course of things we always do, among the people we know best?

Our temptations seldom come in a crisis. They come most often tangled in deceptively casual events, in the usual places, more often than not wearing a familiar face. In fact, the face which temptation most often wears is our own. The most difficult temptation comes from within. It's whatever shakes our confidence in God's powerful love for us and leads us to find our reassurance somewhere else. It's whatever causes us to doubt God's noble purpose for our lives and makes us consider settling for something less faithful and fulfilling.

It's rarely a decision made in one moment. It's a path we gradually set upon. We try to prove our self-worth by throwing ourselves more and more into our work. We begin to drink a little more, just a little more, or try drugs to forget or remember or do whatever we can to help us to believe we're only the victims of circumstances beyond our control. We seek new laughter outside our marriage to convince ourselves we're still special. Or gradually we retreat into the small spaces of our lives, believing if we shut out the world around us we can avoid the pain within us.

Let it be the task of our Lenten journey this year to seek by repentance, fasting, prayer, and the works of love to surrender our lives. Why should we seek to be in control of our lives when we have such a good and gracious God offering to be our Lord? That's the faithful and needed response in both the garden and the desert: to let God be God. To let God be *our* God.

With God's help, let us unravel ordinary events, test familiar impulses, unmask our habits and routines and learn whether our lives are growing in the love and grace and goodness of God, or whether we're drifting or driven somewhere else. Our faith is meant to guide and keep us in the most usual moments and places, as well as in our crises; besides, that's how most of our crises begin.

Alert to temptation in such customary circumstances, we will also be more keenly aware of the thousands of moments of beauty and forgiveness and affection and peace and grace which also make their daily appearance in our lives.

So, this Lent, let's walk the steps of the garden path together.

Lent 2
Genesis 12:1-4a

God Works Wanders

"God works wanders." I read again the Christmas letter from an old friend of the family, typed in this computer age on some ancient typewriter. Surely it was a typo. Looking back over his life, he meant to say, "God works wonders." And surely God does work wonders. But he works wanders too. I found myself reflecting, as our elderly friend had done, on the changes of the years.

God works wanders. Abram and Sarai must have believed that, too. Seventy-five years old, he is asked — commanded — to leave his country, his people, his home. He isn't told where he is going. There are no four-color brochures to lure them there. The wilderness stretches wide before them, as Abram and Sarai and their little company set out.

Did their friends and family walk with them to a rise in the road and then wave and weep and watch until they disappeared from sight? Such a momentous decision and promise is told in so few words. There's nothing of what they felt, what they thought. That would be the fascination of a modern writer and reader. It's enough to tell of God's command and promise, and of Abram's and Sarai's obedient response.

Still, we can easily imagine Abram and Sarai some weeks later wondering whether they were being faithful and wise, or whether they were just foolish and deluded. Sarai wakes, reaches for her husband, but he's not there. She peers outside the tent and sees him sitting by the faintly smoldering fire and goes to his side. "Abram?" "I couldn't sleep," he says. "I'm 75 years old! What great nation can we parent, when we've not yet had our first child? How can my name be great, coming to an unknown land? And how can we be a blessing, even as far as the seas?" "I know," she whispers, "I know. Should we go back?" "No. There's no going back." "Good," Sarai says, "I was hoping you would say that." They stare at the stars a long time before they close their eyes in sleep.

Listen? Do you hear God calling you? "Go," He says, "from your familiar pain and trouble and come to a new spirit which I will show you." This is a journey not measured in miles, of course, but in the Lenten disciplines of reflection, repentance, and renewal.

As the prefixes remind us (*re*flection, *re*pentance, *re*newal), this is not a journey we're venturing upon for the first time. Nor will it be the last. Each year brings its changes and we face new challenges. Old Abram and Sarai were willing to let God lead them into a new life. And in this new life they received new identities, with new names to prove it. Abraham and Sarah put their very lives in his hands. In whose hands do you want to live your life?

It's so easy to stay where we are, even if it's painful, just because it's familiar. Destructive perceptions, abusive habits, hurtful attitudes, broken relationships — all these, no matter how painful they are, are often more comfortable than venturing into a way of thinking and living which will be new to us. Still, God says, come to the place I will show you.

Some of us have held hurts so long we can't imagine life without them. Some we learned very young. Perhaps we grew up in a world where we never were good enough, could never please the people we wanted so desperately to please, never experienced love which we could count on no matter what.

So perhaps we've been blaming everyone else for our troubles. Or we've developed compulsive or obsessive behaviors we are afraid to lose. We eat too much, work too much, drink too much, gossip too much. We may even be risking our jobs, our marriages, our children's respect, our friends' company because we've lost sight of who we really are. We have all these layers to mask our hearts' cries for forgiveness, hope, love. If we don't reach out, we think, if we don't venture forward, we can't ever be rejected again, or fail again.

Still, God says, "Go to the place I will show you." An Arab proverb says, "A journey of a thousand miles begins with a single step." With modest beginnings we surrender our wills and our lives to God.

A small company of travelers leaves one little village of an unknown name in a forgotten country. And yet, from that quiet beginning, of which the world took no notice, began the story of God entering history by his covenant with one nation and then, in the fullness of time, by the new covenant given in Christ to the whole world.

So don't apologize for your modest beginnings. One day this week one of you will begin to belittle your spouse, feeling frustrated with your job, and stop and walk away — a beginning. In another home a man will reach for a bottle, hesitate, and close the cupboard — not the last drink, but a beginning. In another home a brother will phone the sister from whom he's been estranged for years, saying, "I want us to talk. It won't be an old argument" — a beginning.

It may feel strange to seek to be so intentional, reflective, about our lives. We're used to following our too familiar patterns, even though sometimes we've stood back and looked at our lives and realized our actions made no sense at all. We have been protecting that which hurts us, putting at risk what we cherish most. Not all our lives are so imperiled, but those which are must be challenged to make this Lent a time of courageous pilgrimage. It's a pilgrimage to new life in Christ, our own easter.

Those among us whose lives are more whole need to deepen our sense of humility. Perhaps we haven't faced the same challenges in our lives. Perhaps we wrestled with our own deepest pain long ago, and now are supportive of others with our encouragement and prayers. Or perhaps our greatest challenge is yet unknown and still ahead of us. Nevertheless, all of us can grow in our trust of God to lead and guide us. We have the scriptures and the sacraments to feed us. And, too, we have this company, this congregation to travel with us.

One never knows what's beginning and what's ending. Looking back we may, or we may not, be able to recall the insignificant little events — a passing comment, a glance across a room, words on the page of a book, a thought as we stared out a window — minor events which were the beginnings of something which shaped a significant aspect of our lives. What loving gesture, repentant prayer, word spoken or purposely not spoken, what discipline exercised, might indicate a new beginning in your spiritual life this week? Once, an elderly couple, hearts quickened by the promises of a living and gracious God, packed their belongings and set out with their family for a promised future.

God works wanders!

Lent 3
Exodus 17:1-7

God's A Catcher

Amid all the exotic sights and excitement of a circus there's one moment which for me holds more daring, beauty and grace than any other. A moment when the clowns cease their pratfalls, while tigers pace and snarl in their cages, elephants shift their bulk from side to side, the ringmaster hushes the crowd, and cross-pathed spotlights illumine upturned faces in scattered circles around the arena as they focus high, high above the ground.

The moment is this: an aerialist lets go of the trapeze and sails and turns, even tumbles, in mid-air. That's the moment. In seconds the flyer will be in the hands of the catcher, who has timed the swing of his trapeze in such a balance against the motion of the flyer — a pattern not easily discernible to the audience — that he will be in just the right place at exactly the right time to grasp the flyer's arms. That moment (trusting, precarious, graceful) is the lifetime (faithful, challenging, full of grace) of a Christian.

We have accepted the love of God and across the years have sought to live in faith. But the absolute certainty of our faith is beyond this world. In the meantime we are on our journey, having ventured forward, as we said last week, in faith, toward an unknown future. This then is our Lenten journey and our life's journey — to always be leaving that which has been for what we have not yet known.

We shouldn't be surprised that the life of the believer is not static and still. God did not create the world to work that way. Do we too much take for granted the changes of this season all around us? Don't say that this spring the flowers will bloom again, for the flowers which will bloom in your yard are flowers which neither you nor the world has ever seen before. Each leaf on the trees will make its appearance for the very first time. Even the rocks which seem to us unchanging only seem so because of the brevity of our observation.

So too our faith is not lived in the security of everything familiar all over again, but in the reality of the chances and changes of each new day. John Updike writes in a foreword to one of his books, "At all times, an old world is collapsing and a new world is arising; we have better eyes for the collapse than the rise, for the old one is the world we know."

We often wish we had not ventured forth. Listen to the Hebrews, on their way, they knew, to their promised land. They were very thirsty, and complained to Moses, "Why did you bring us out of Egypt to kill us and our children and our livestock with thirst?"

Could they have been thinking wistfully about their years of slavery in Egypt? At least there they had food to eat and water to drink. They longed for the world they had known and understood, even though it was a life of bondage. Of course, at this moment, they were likely forgetting the depth of pain, danger, and humiliation of their lives there. And in their present challenges they were forgetting the grandeur of the promises God had made to them as a people. Foolish people.

Or notice the man healed by Jesus in today's gospel. Don't you suppose he had always assumed his troubles would be over if only he could see? Yet once healed he is subject to a barrage of questions by the townsfolk and by the Pharisees. Even his parents distance themselves enough to let him be interrogated by their suspicious neighbors. Unsatisfied with his answers, those who ran that village cast him out. To an outcast, perhaps blindness wasn't so bad after all. Foolish man.

You wouldn't catch us bitter for new challenges. We'd never long for old sins. Or would we? Last week we spoke of the need to trust that God has called us to leave those aspects of our lives which are hurtful to us and others, and to trust in his guidance and grace.

Does that mean that our lives are then easier? No. In fact, as for the Hebrews, it is often more difficult. At least it seems more difficult because we have new challenges and because we can forget so easily how painful things really were.

The member of a family who has been used to being belittled, who asserts her new self-image as a precious child of God, will not automatically have the family's respect and appreciation. In fact, it's likely to be just the opposite. She'll feel she doesn't fit in. They may well ridicule her new self-image. And they may not compensate her with the kind of conditional acceptance they gave her before.

A person who seeks to give up a compulsive or addictive behavior finds his determination constantly challenged. It's not only the addiction itself. Old friends may feel threatened by his change of habits. Even people who objected to his behavior may feel threatened by his new self-control. He may have been so sure that life would all fall into place that, as challenges mount, he doubts himself and his new direction.

Or perhaps our problem isn't that we're tempted to return to the past, but that we are altogether focused on something in the future, the imagined end of our striving. We think everything will be all right once we get a new job, once we get married, have children, or once we've put our children through college, or once we get that house of which we've always dreamed, or once we retire.

The reality is that life is the journey wherever we are. We live in the time in between. It's not as familiar as time in the past, nor as ideal as some imaginary time in the future, but it is the reality in which we live. And it's a time full of opportunities for God to show us his grace.

Look again at the Hebrews in the wilderness. They had a real problem. They really were thirsty. More than thirsty, they feared for their lives and the lives of their children and their stock. God doesn't punish them. He doesn't send them back to Egypt to live in the familiar pain of their slavery, to get what they deserve.

No, when Moses cries out to God, God leads him and some of the elders to a rock. Striking the rock with a stick, water pours forth. God provides for their need.

And pay attention to what happens when Jesus hears that the man of our gospel, once blind, has been cast out. He searches for him. Having found him, he establishes with him an eternal relationship. To this man, he is no longer simply a prophet, or even a healer. He is his Lord. And the man worships him. Jesus did not heal and desert him.

Nor will he fail to provide and care for us. Of course, it may not always be when and how and as we expect. Not only does he provide us with food and clothing, home and family (though we dare never take these precious gifts for granted), but also he provides for us the constant reassurance of his abiding love and forgiveness, his gifts of discernment and determination, the strength and nurture of the gospel and the sacraments, the power and pleasure of his presence.

Dear friends, we are on a journey. Our lives are full of so many changes. Some of us are still recovering from the last great challenge to our faith: a frightening prognosis for our health, the death of someone who has given our lives deep joy and stability, a severe threat to our relationship with our spouse or our children or our parents, some staggering blow to our job or career. Others of us are still in the midst of crisis. For others of us, some unknown challenge lies ahead.

But this is where we live. We are here because we have recognized that our lives are not our own, that we belong to God, and we're grateful. We have responded to his call to follow in faith our Lord. We now seek to live by his grace, his love beyond all our deserving on this life journey. How do we do this? It's our Lenten focus. And it's the challenge of our lifetime.

In mid-air we are suspended. No longer hanging on only to what we have seen and touched, but trusting in the promises God has made known to us in Jesus Christ. There's no spotlight on this venture, to hold us up for flattery or ridicule. There's only the light of God's love in which we live and move. And if it seems we are flyers, suspended in the air, reaching by faith, then know that

God is the unfailing Catcher. And if it sometimes seems we are flying through life's air without support, by faith we know that, invisible to the world and more often than not also to us, God has already caught us in his arms.

Lent 4
1 Samuel 16:1-13

In The Eyes Of God

Consider how differently you've felt before another person's eyes. Think how you may have withered under the stare of an angry teacher. How your head may have begun to swim in the dreamy gaze of a lover. How belittled you felt as your boss seemed to look right through you without seeing you. Or how you could have burst with joy in the proud eyes of your parents.

How differently we can feel in another person's eyes. And how differently eyes can see us — differences not dependent on optical issues, but on concerns of the heart. Eyes reveal much of a person's mood, even one's nature. We've lots of words for people's eyes: twinkling eyes, beady eyes, bedroom eyes, piercing eyes, shifty eyes. We're affected by the eyes that look upon us. Sometimes it makes all the difference in the world.

Craig, only three years old, spills his milk, and his father says, "I can't believe how clumsy you are. Can't you ever do anything right?" And through the years, told over and over of his stupidity and worthlessness, he comes to believe it. Now Craig is a very unhappy adult, who's learned to make countless excuses for himself and is quick to find fault with everyone else, wanting no one to be better than he is.

In a nursing home, a frail, little woman named Carrie asks

for a bedpan. An aide breezes through the room, her eyes on the television which, like all the others on the hall, is tuned to her favorite soap. Never looking at the frail woman squirming in the bed, she says, "Hi, sweetie, don't you look beautiful today! Whatever it is, I'll be back in a few minutes." Under the covers Carrie is only a fraction of the person she used to be. In her mind, she begins to fear she's disappearing altogether.

What a difference a gaze makes!

Israel needs a new king, and Samuel will anoint the Lord's chosen. God sends Samuel to Bethlehem, for he will provide a king from among the sons of Jesse. Samuel meets the first of Jesse's eight sons. Eliab, he thinks, has qualities which could make him a good king. Most likely he was the oldest. Perhaps he was strong and tall, perhaps he seemed wise and self-assured. But the Lord told him it was not to be Eliab. Then perhaps Abinidab or Shammah? No. Jesse sends in four more sons. None of them, either. There must have been fine qualities in some of these men. Still, Samuel knows the Lord has chosen none of these. Is there anyone else? Jesse answers, "Just my youngest, but we left him to watch the sheep."

Samuel asks Jesse to send for him, and when he comes in, he is handsome, with a ruddy complexion and sparkling eyes. This is the one, the Lord tells Samuel. But it isn't a matter of his comely appearance. God had said to Samuel, "Don't look at his face or his height. I don't see as people see. They see only the outward appearance. I see a person's heart." The Lord saw something deeper in this young boy fresh from the sheepfold. His was the heart of a king, the greatest king ever to reign over Israel. This was David.

Many generations later the wonder was told that there was to be a new king born in the town of Bethlehem, of the House of David. This king would be a king greater even than David. We don't know if the eyes of this promised King sparkled or not. But we do know that as he began his gentle reign he did not see people as other people saw them; his eyes, like the eyes of God, looked into their hearts.

These are the eyes which spotted a curious tax collector in a sycamore, noticed disappointed little children behind his disciples' robes; eyes which pierced Peter's heart in the firelight of a courtyard; eyes which had compassion on his mother even from the cross. It goes beyond a keen sense of observation. It was a matter of seeing what nobody else, looking upon the same person, would see.

In the midst of our Lenten journey, God doesn't see us as everyone else sees us. People around us may see us as cool, successful, unattractive, popular, old, whatever. It doesn't matter at all how others may see us. God sees our hearts, sees us as we really are. Perhaps we wish we had him fooled, like those we've led to believe that we're less frightened, more confident, happier than we really are. Or perhaps we're deeply grateful that God sees through all the shallow, negative judgments which so many people have placed on us. Probably it's both.

Our Lord, to our joy and to our sorrow, looks into our hearts and sees us as we really are. In Lent, that's a call for introspection. To confess that we have not loved our Lord with our whole hearts, nor loved our neighbors as ourselves.

In Lent, it's especially important that we confess our sinfulness as specifically as we're able. In what ways have we failed God and ourselves? Because we can't hide from God, we dare not use all our usual ways to avoid our sinfulness. We're used to denying our sins, minimizing them, excusing them, blaming them on others. This Lent, let's examine ourselves, asking God to search our hearts. We benefit from naming our sins, our needs, and losses, and failings. And we admit to God that only by his grace and guidance can we find healing and help.

Marvelously, even when we make ourselves so vulnerable to God, we discover he loves us no less. Like the Psalmist, we may fall asleep praying, "Lord, you know everything I do and feel and think...Your knowledge of me is so deep, it is beyond my understanding." And yet even so completely revealed we may be confident that in the morning "when I awake, I am still with you, O God" (Psalm 139).

The eyes of God, searching our hearts, do more than see us as we really are. God's eyes see in us the person each is becoming. God sees us more loving, more whole, more forgiving, more hopeful, more kind and joyful than ever we have been. And, we pray, by God's grace, that is the person we are becoming.

This Christ lives in us. Through him, we also can do more than see others as the world sees them. We can strive to see others as God would see them. It won't be so easy to write them off. We'll see each other with a significantly greater degree of humility, of compassion, of empathy, of tolerance and acceptance. That's a wisdom we apply not only to individuals but also to groups — blacks, whites, Mexicans, the old, the young, the poor, the rich, any group of people we are tempted to label together. Who are each of these persons really? Through the eyes of Christ we know that it has little to do with what we use to categorize them together, and everything to do with what God sees in their hearts.

In the shepherd boy the Lord saw the King for his people. In the rough-handed fishermen he saw men who could not only pull nets from the night sea, but could reach for people in the dark nights of their souls. Even as they foolishly quarrel about greatness in the kingdom, Jesus sees in one the willingness to be the first of the twelve to suffer a martyr's death, and in the other a recipient for a powerful vision on the island of Patmos.

Now, when God looks into your hearts what does he see, of all that has been, and all that is yet to be?

One poetic believer, Gerard Manley Hopkins, wrote that the Christian

> *Acts in God's eyes what in God's eyes he is: Christ.*
> *For Christ plays in ten thousand places,*
> *Lovely in limbs, and lovely in eyes not his,*
> *To the Father, through the features of men's faces.*
> (from "Kingfishers Catch Fire")

Lent 5
Ezekiel 37:1-14

It Ain't Over 'Til It's Over

Masada is a massive rock, rising from the south Judean desert. Walking round the edge of its flattened height, there is no life to be seen anywhere. All around, only the expanse of the dry, rocky desert. Except for the Sea to the west. Yet this is the salt-soaked Dead Sea whose water is lifeless, absolutely lifeless.

On this mount Herod had built a fortress for escape. Later, nearly a thousand Jewish Zealots made their home there to keep the pure faith and to elude the Romans. On the eastern corner of Masada, facing distant and unseen Jerusalem, the Zealots had built a synagogue. One of the several scrolls archaeologists found there was that of the prophet Ezekiel.

I marvel to think of those eyes scanning the vast Judean desert, listening to Ezekiel tell of being set in a valley, a valley full of bones. The bones were many and the bones were very dry. The Lord asked Ezekiel, "Can these bones live?" And Ezekiel, avoiding the obvious answer (which was surely "no"), said wonderingly, "Lord, you know better than I."

When the Roman legions entered the fortress of Masada after a siege of three years, Josephus tells that they found the bodies of almost a thousand Zealots, men, women and children together, preferring death to slavery. Death in the valley, death in the sea, and death on the rocky tabletop above the desert.

The words of Ezekiel dated from another period of conflict and warfare in the history of the Hebrew people. They were in exile in Babylon, Ezekiel among them. Jerusalem had fallen to a great nation contending with other great nations. Jerusalem and the people of Judah were only bit players in this military contest. But not to Ezekiel. Not to God.

Having condemned his people for their unfaithfulness, Ezekiel now proclaimed that God would return his people to their homeland and that Israel would become his instrument of salvation for all the earth. Return from exile they did, but glory eluded them as a nation. After the Babylonians, there was Alexander the Great and the Greeks, then the Romans. But for a few brief years of freedom under the Macabees, the nation of Israel was a conquered land, even as they were in the time of the Zealots on Masada, and their doomed resistance to the Romans.

"Can these bones live?" "Lord, you know." What is the life we hope for? Where is fulfilled Ezekiel's vision of life out of death?

Several miles outside Jerusalem in the town of Bethany, lived Jesus' friends Mary, Martha and Lazarus. Often he stayed there, even as he would the last week of his life, walking outside the city walls of Jerusalem the several miles to their home in Bethany to sleep.

The sisters send word to Jesus in Galilee that Lazarus is sick, even dying. As Jesus comes down the dusty road to Bethany, Martha hurries to meet him. With a heavy heart she greets him reproachingly, "Lord, if you had been here my brother would not have died." And then she adds hopefully, "Yet even now I know whatever you ask of God, God will give it to you." ("Can these bones live?" "Lord, you know better than I.")

Jesus reassures her with the widespread belief in the resurrection which will follow a person's death, as taught by the Pharisees. "Your brother," Jesus says, "will rise again." I hear Martha sigh, only marginally satisfied to know that Lazarus, gone from her hearth and table, will have life after death.

It's the same sigh we all breathe for those we've loved and lost, grateful for the promise of their resurrection to another world, but deeply feeling the sorrow of our helplessness and hopelessness in this world.

What Jesus says next is not the faint reassurance of familiar doctrine about the future. Had he said what he is about to say that day in their home when Mary sat at his feet, and had Martha heard it bustling in the kitchen, the pots and pans in her hands would have clattered to the floor. This is new to Martha, and new upon the earth.

Listen to him. Piercing her heart, and the hearts of believers forever, he states, "I am the resurrection and the life, whoever believes in me, though he dies, yet shall he live and whoever lives and believes in me will never die." Now, even now, "I am the resurrection." Martha is taken aback, but by grace she knows it is true: "I believe that you are the Christ, the Son of God, the one who is coming into the world."

Into the world! Hope belongs not only to some other realm but to this world in which she and Mary and you and I all live! The raising of Lazarus then is not, of course, the promise that we and our loved ones will be returned after death to this world. Lazarus again will die. As Martha and Mary and you and I and all of us will die. Our Lord raises Lazarus to show that all power in life and death belongs to him — even *in* this world!

Such a gospel thunders against the hopelessness we too often feel before the greater and lesser crises of our life. People pat us on the backs and say, "You can't do anything about it, get used to it." We feel scattered, disconnected, dry. Can these bones live? Around us hangs the heavy weight of "no." We feel trapped, in the dark, behind a great obstacle. Around us seems to hang the stench of "too late." Smugly or sadly, the world watches and waits for things to take their usual course and reach their predictable end.

It's the bottom of the ninth inning. The home team is losing 8 to 4. There are two outs, and with a man on second, they begin the lower half of the batting order. Fans are already filing toward the aisles and pouring down the ramps into the parking lot. One of the men on the bench calls to the coach, "Hey, we'll get 'em tomorrow." Without taking his eyes off the field, the coach retorts, "It ain't over 'til it's over!"

It's so easy to lose heart and hope, to assume that things have gone too far. It's too late; there's nowhere to turn. To assume it's over.

Becky drives away from her doctor's office, fighting the tears. Having felt as though everything depended on having another child, the result of the test is overwhelming: she'll never be pregnant again.

Ben stares out the third-story window of his office building, weary of his work, bored with his life, remembering springtimes filled with baseball mitts and old carburetors, with love notes and pretty girls. And now he's not looking forward to anything.

Mandy reaches behind the jumbled spices for her pills, hands shaking. All she wants is enough to get herself relaxed before the kids get home from school. Maybe she'll go to a meeting again in the fall. Or when the kids are older. Or when... there was another good excuse, but she can't recall it just then.

Obed is washing blood from the floor of a church in Rwanda. His brother was killed in the slaughter. He sent his wife and children with those who were fleeing and he's not heard from her since. He stares at the floor. The blood's not coming up; it's in too deep.

Against such despair the church proclaims that the love and power of God in Christ Jesus is come into the world. Our hope is not reserved for another day, another life, another world. Can these bones live? By the grace of God, the answer is surely "yes." We have the power to change, grow, gain control, find acceptance, be comforted, gather strength, whatever we need to renew and rebuild our lives.

It's true that life holds its real losses and every day holds its genuine endings. The last batter strikes out, and the lights go off in the stadium. The curtain closes in front of you or the door shuts behind you. Day drifts into dusk and dark.

Not always will we experience the reversal of our losses. Jesus wept at Lazarus' grave, and we too weep. We cry understandable tears for the girlfriend lost, the baby not born, the career that faltered, the grip of addiction, the death of a friend, the devastation of violence and injustice.

But we need not despair. The Christ who lives in us *is* the resurrection and *is* the life. Meaning, promise, and purpose can't be held hostage to the limits of the conventional wisdom surrounding us or to the narrowness of our own experience.

Can these bones live? Listen to the rattling across the valleys of our lives. We who have our hope in Christ live in him, and we can take hope and give it to one another, and to others beyond. Now, as we take the last steps on this Lenten journey, let us all continue to draw closer to God, seeking his will for our lives and the power to bring it to life.

Can these bones live? Ours? Lord, you know. Now we know too. "Yes, Lord, I believe you are the Christ, Son of the living God, coming into the world." And into my world, my life.

Passion/Palm Sunday
Isaiah 50:4-9a

Our Champion Rides Into Battle

From the battlement, the watchman sees a knight riding from the forest and ascending the hill. He is in full armor, a long lance in one arm, a great shield in the other. His powerful black charger wears a coat of bright red and paws the air and snorts as the rider reins him in at the castle gate. The knight bangs his lance on the mighty doors and shouts his challenge: "Who will contend with me? Let us face one another. Who dares to be my opponent? Let him present himself!"

Day by day a giant from the ranks of the Philistines rises and dons his bronze helmet and a coat of mail, weighing itself as much as some men. He slings a bronze javelin over his shoulder and takes his spear with a shaft like a 2 by 4 and a 15-pound iron head. Across the Valley of Elah he taunts the Israelites, encamped on the other side. "Choose a man for yourselves and let him come down to me. I defy the ranks of Israel! Give me a man so that we may fight together!"

A Chippewa brave crosses the frozen lake on his pony. War feathers, braids and blanket, tail and mane all iced by the north wind. To the edge of the Sioux encampment he rides. "It's a good day to die! Only the earth lasts forever!" He throws his spear into the camp and from his pony pacing against the snow-burdened pines, calls, "Who is my enemy? He who killed my brother in the hunting party two days ago. Let him come forth to fight!"

The sleek silver car squeals around the corner and skids to a stop at the end of the street. Men under the street lamp turn and reach toward guns and knives hidden in their jackets. Children run behind doors and fences. Windows shut and porch lights are snuffed. A young man steps from the car, armed with an automatic rifle. He raises it in the air as he shouts, "This street belongs to me! If anyone wants to argue that, he can show himself and we'll settle it right now!"

From the ramparts of a city, another cluster of anxious observers gauged the threat of their enemy's approach: a lone rider, presenting himself for battle — the final battle.

> *"Who will contend with me?*
> *Let us stand up together.*
> *Who is my adversary?*
> *Let him come near to me!"*

On a donkey he rode, his face set like flint, advancing on Jerusalem. From the ramparts of the city walls and from the temple mount, watched Roman officers, priests and temple guards, officials of the court.

How threatening could he have seemed, this rabbi on the donkey? Even so, if there was a battle to be waged, they were ready. The priests had the temple treasury and their skill at manipulating the sacred law. The Romans had their legions of soldiers with chariots and swords and spears. The court officials wielded the authority of the Emperor and power over life and death.

Still, there was something unsettling about the response of the crowds. They were singing and shouting, "Hosanna!" Some were climbing the trees and cutting palms to place in his path. Others took off their coats to muffle the dust on the road before him. But this was a crowd which had come to the city for a holiday; as they could be so easily swayed this day, this way, so they could be swayed another day, another way. "Who is this again?"

"This is the prophet Jesus from Nazareth of Galilee," shouts the crowd in the streets. You and I have invited this donkey-riding warrior to be our King, to go into battle before us.

We have this Lent named our adversaries: all that tempts, tears and traps our hearts. Each of us has, in our own way, made our own commitments to begin this renewal, ventured toward our promised but unknown futures, sought to give the power for the direction of our lives to God. We've struggled to accept the opposition to our resolve, and worked to see ourselves in the love of God and to see the persons we are by God's grace becoming. We gathered strength and hope in knowing that the power of God is not reserved for some future forever, but that the resurrected Christ with all his gentle might comes even now into our family life, our study, our employment, our friendships, our leisure, our hearts.

What weapons are ours under this Warrior King? We'd better realize that if we seek to do battle with our adversaries on their terms, with their choice of weapons, we have deserted our captain. And we will fail.

For the weapons promised us for this war are not those prized in the world around us. We will not be doing battle with the weapons of deceit, violence, manipulation, blame, ridicule and self-pity. Our weapons will be those of the spirit of God. Earlier in the book of Isaiah, the gifts of the spirit are named this way: wisdom and understanding, counsel and might, knowledge and the fear of the Lord, the spirit of joy in his presence.

Don't be misled by the seeming advantage of the powers of darkness. That day, that deceptively bright and happy day when Jesus rode through the city gate, the fate of the power of evil was already sealed. To be sure, betrayal, suffering, and death soon beat back the prophet from Galilee. But in seven days' dawning, the whole world would never be the same, with the dawn of the reign of grace.

Here is the servant promised in Isaiah's song, our first lesson this morning. Jesus is the Messiah who wakened each day with the voice of God in his ear, and more than that, in his heart. This is he who sustained with a word those who were weary, saying, "Come to me all you who are weary and carrying heavy burdens and I will give you rest." And more than words he gave them. He is the example of one who finds strength in God even when one's own strength is depleted. This is he who submitted to the insults and abuse of those most threatened by the freedom of the gospel. This is the one who now sets his face like flint toward Jerusalem, towards the religious, political and military opposition which waited for him there. This is the one who rides into the city ready to do battle. The servant song of Isaiah may not have been spoken that day, but its fulfilled prophecy is woven into the shouts of the crowd, the excitement of the disciples, the wariness of the authorities, the beat of the donkey's hooves and the profound silence of the solitary rider. "Who will contend with me? Let us stand up together. Who is my adversary? Let him come near to me."

Who is his adversary? Enemies were not difficult to identify. In the religious realm there is Caiaphas. In the political and military realms, Pilate and Herod. And all those who served them and their purposes.

Who is his adversary? More than any of these, it is the one whose purposes all of them serve, the one with whom he contended in the desert. Now they would do battle again. Deep within, the Warrior King on the donkey knows he has an all-righteous and all-powerful ally. "Behold, the Lord God helps me. Who will declare me guilty?"

In this age when kings no longer lead their armies into battle, our King still promises his presence with us as we contend with all that truly challenges our lives, our faith, our trust in the grace of God within us. In so many ways we do battle each day. It may seem so unlikely a battleground: the hall outside our office, the kitchen table, the school bus, any of the thousand places we find ourselves each week.

And what is the battle in which we're engaged? We may think we know. It may be a battle to succeed, to be liked, to be accomplished, to be happy. Or maybe it's a battle to survive, to provide for ourselves and those we love. Those battles are very real. And they are too much a part of the human spirit to dismiss them altogether.

But, of far greater importance, is the battle for our spirits. If we are alert, there are countless challenges everyday to the faith that lives within us. There are so many ways we are daily tempted or assaulted to let our confidence in the love of God be shaken.

This is the love that gives us peace, wholeness, life. This is the love that makes us truly human, that enables us to fulfill the deepest purposes our lives could hold. In comparison to this war, battles for popularity, success, power, even survival, pale in significance.

With armor and weapons and allies the world little understands, our Lord attacks the powers of darkness, leading the final charge with no troops following after. It is one of those battles in which the observers need to watch for the dust to clear and the casualties to be counted before victory can be claimed. By Friday of this week the enemies of God and grace will assume their triumph, but the sunrise of Easter dawn will reveal our victorious Lord.

This Lord is our Warrior King. He calls us to be his witnesses, to share in his victory and to invite others to join in its victory, too. This will be our Easter theme — to focus on the spiritual gifts God gives us for this warfare of our whole lifetime. But not beyond our lifetime. For then the battle is done and the victory won also in us.

Is it possible to wage war with such weapons, even in this modern world of ours? An event only a few years ago provides a wondrous story. The movement to topple the Berlin Wall began in the churches of East Germany. One of the central churches in this activism was St. Nicholas Lutheran Church in Leipzig, where Luther preached and Bach played the organ. As the movement grew, there were evening prayer services. One particular night, not only were hundreds entering the church for prayer but thousands were gathering on the street outside. Seeing such a large crowd forming and well aware of the potentially explosive situation, the communist government moved troops into place according to its contingency plans.

Inside the church the pastor led the congregation in prayers for freedom and peace, praying for the destruction of the Berlin Wall and all barriers to freedom but also for nonviolence, especially that night. As the people came out and joined the demonstration, thousands of candles were passed around — so many that it took two hands to hold them all. Soon the inner city ring street was circled with burning candles, the singing of songs and hymns, the offering of prayers. There was no riot, and the police did not move in to disperse the crowd. It was not long until the movement succeeded and the hated wall came down.

Afterward the chief of police commented, "We were prepared for anything that night, for everything. Everything except candles and prayers."

Never underestimate the power of the grace of God and the gifts of the Spirit. With such power Christ, as our champion, rode into Jerusalem that day of passion and palms. Such power is ours, too, for the great crises of our day and for the ordinary struggles of our daily lives.

There's a hymn we never sing this day but which uses such imagery to describe our Warrior King, our Champion.

> *The old satanic foe / Has sworn to work us woe!*
> *With craft and dreadful might / He arms himself to fight.*
> *On earth he has no equal.*
>
> *No strength of ours can match his might. / We would be lost, rejected.*
> *But now a champion comes to fight, / Whom God himself elected.*
>
> ...
> *Christ Jesus, mighty Lord, / God's only Son, adored.*
> *He holds the field victorious.*
>
> *God's Word forever shall abide, / No thanks to foes who fear it;*
> *For God himself fights by our side / With weapons of the Spirit.*
>
> ...
> *The Kingdom's ours forever!*
> (from "A Mighty Fortress" by Martin Luther)

Maundy Thursday
Exodus 12:1-4 (5-10) 11-14

A Cross For A Doorpost

Lambs! More lambs! We need more lambs! Let the blood from each lamb flow into a pool and the pools into streams and the streams into rivers! Bring trains to take it to the cities! Ready ships to carry it across the world!

What did the scriptures say? Blood on the doorposts and on the lintel? And those in that home shall be spared?

Then take paintbrushes to the doorposts of the homes where the little children are knocked across the floor. Soak with blood the doorways of the shock trauma and coronary care units, and the AIDS hospices too. Smear it on the walls by the heating grates and on the arches of the underpasses where the homeless sleep. Cover with lambs' blood the spans of the bridge in the midst of the earthquake or the path of the tornado. Drench the awnings in the marketplace before the rockets fall, and pour blood on the rooftop of the car in which a bomb is planted at the federal building. Around and through the teeming refugee camps paint the trees and rocks, and if there are no rocks or trees then color red the clouds.

Why wasn't there lambs' blood on the sliding doors of the boxcars headed for Auschwitz and Treblinka, or on the heavy glass doors of the skyscraper before the raging fire? Why not on the wheel of the barley wagon before it broke the little girl?

Who doesn't ache to read that God gave the Hebrew slaves in Egypt a key to keep their lives when the angel of death passed over the land? Why isn't there such an answer to our fervent prayers, as we pray for the safety of our children, for the healing of our friend, for the survival of a town in the path of a storm, a nation torn by war, or a land besieged by famine?

There's an aspect of this ancient story which causes me, I confess, to slip by its central point and its unique salvation history and long for such a life-sparing promise for our loved ones and for strangers the world over.

But the promise is not there. For all our fervent attention to staying alive, we do not find in scripture a formula to spare us from death's threat. Everyone in all the Bible stories dies. Sometimes they are spared for a time; there is a purpose to be accomplished in witness to God's redemption in the history of his people — as with the Hebrews escaping Egypt, or Shadrach, Meshach, and Abednego in the fiery furnace, or Lazarus in his hillside tomb. For God's purposes, and for compassion, their lives were spared. At least for that night, or that day.

At the table, on the night he was betrayed, this night before his death, Jesus is not making any promises about a way to stay alive in the midst of so many dangers. In fact, he is doing the opposite.

How could he promise them that in the hour in which death would most threaten them that there was a formula by which they could be spared? He wanted them to understand, though it was yet beyond their comprehension, that in the hour when death threatened him, he would die. And that hour was soon.

On a cross he would die a cruel and public death. His eyes would close for the last time, he would breathe his last breath and his heart would cease beating. How could he hold out to them any promise of having their lives spared?

He had tried to prepare them not only for the dangers which draw or drive every person into death, but for the particular threat to their lives as witnesses to the gospel. "Blessed are you," he affirmed and admonished them, "when people revile you and persecute you and utter all kinds of evil against you falsely on my account...in the same way they persecuted the prophets who were before you." He meant that many of these prophets died in the cause of their calling. According to tradition, martyrdom awaited all of the eleven save one.

No, Jesus isn't speaking of sparing lives. It's not sparing them from death that he's talking about; it's love. Love is the focus, and it gives this day its name. "Maundy" derives from "commandment." So in our gospel, Jesus is summarizing all he has said and done and been in these words: "A new commandment I give to you, that you love one another; even as I have loved you, that you love one another."

None of this need dim the wonder of that ancient redemptive event. God had promised that the children of Abraham and Sarah would become a great nation, and that the salvation history which began with their journey from Haran would not be thwarted.

Driven by famine, succeeding generations migrated to Egypt and across the passing years were reduced to forced labor, living like slaves. In Moses, God provided leadership for their escape. The last of the plagues, the midnight death of the first-born throughout the land, posed the greatest danger. By the sign of the lambs' blood on the doorposts and lintels of their homes, the Israelites were spared for escape. This hasty departure enabled them to reach the sea before the army of the pharaoh. Through the parted waters they headed for the wilderness on the other side and the promised land beyond. When the sea closed upon the pharaoh's chariots behind them, their escape was accomplished, and their holy destiny secure, at least that far. With the Passover supper they would ever after remember their exodus and God's redemption.

But there would always be other chariots, other armies, other seas. As there will always be more earthquakes and hurricanes, floods and fires, plagues and diseases, and dangers on country lanes and in city streets. The redemptive story of the exodus is the promise that God would continue to work through this people the salvation which would be the hope of the whole world.

As we hear the story of the first Passover, we remember Jesus and the twelve sharing their Passover supper. No more is it a matter of escaping pharaohs and kings, of evading soldiers and their weapons. In fact, this is the night of his betrayal, the night before he would submit to the sentence of petty rulers, be subjected to the cruelty of forgotten soldiers and be executed high on a hill called the Skull.

Yet what was accomplished in that death was not just the continuing of the redemptive story but its climax. His death is the proclamation of the redemption God wills for the world. The grace of God, his unbounded and undeserved love for the world, is greater than all our violence, our self-fascination, our rejection of him. Even as the world nails him to the cross, Jesus proclaims the love of God for the world. "He who did not withhold his own son, but gave him up for all of us, will he not with him give us everything else?" (Romans 8). This redemption, this grace, this love for the world, beloved, is given and shed for *you*.

As the twelve sat with him at the table they heard the promise but could not yet fully take it in. Still, he gives them an assurance which we have never forgotten. "When you eat this bread and drink this cup in my name," he promised, "I will be present in you even as I am with you now."

There are not enough lambs to provide sufficient blood for the doorposts of the world. But the blood of Christ, shed on the cross, is more than enough for all the doorposts through all ages until the end.

It is not the promise that we shall not die, for we shall, all of us. But the promise, by the grace of God, that "After the first death, there is no other." [1]

---

1. from "A Refusal to Mourn the Death, By Fire, of a Child in London" by Dylan Thomas

Good Friday
Isaiah 52:13—53:12

A Day Like Two Thousand Years

*"Do not ignore this one fact, beloved,
that with the Lord a thousand years are like one day,
and one day like a thousand years."*
Even two thousand.

At 5:30 in the early dawn, on the day of Jesus' death, as he stepped forth into the light from his incarceration to be delivered to the temple military guard, adjusting his eyes to the low slant of the rising sun, a girl on the island of Cyprus was also blinking her eyes as the sun rose over the hill. She whispered, "Good morning, Mother. Good morning, Father. I'll get breakfast today." She went out to the orchard and gathered some oranges, figs and dates for their breakfast. On the way back she picked some flowers for the table.

She set the fruit in a beautiful brass bowl on their carved cedar table. She arranged the yellow and pink flowers in a fine vase. On her lap she carefully unfolded a napkin of cloth woven in Thebes. She told her parents she might ride her horse down to the sea that morning.

As she remarked that the oranges seemed exceptionally tasty, a man leaned in and shouted, "You disgusting excuse for a girl, you took more than your share again!" and hurried out carrying their breakfast. Only there was no fruit, no brass bowl, no napkin, no flowers, no parents. Only Leda. And Leda, 11 years old, is a leper. She'd not seen her father since she came to the leper colony with her mother three years ago. And her mother died last winter. She is exceptionally disfigured for one so young. The rest of the people in the leper colony think she's crazy.

She is, actually. Each morning she leaves her cave and goes to the edge of the colony to get some of the bread left there by people from the village. Often she is accused of taking too much. But she insists that she is taking food enough for three.

She folds a rag from her lap and lays it in the center of a stone slab next to some weeds. "That's all right," she says, "you both can finish the fruit. I'm not really hungry today."

See, my servant shall prosper;
he shall be exalted and lifted up, and shall be very high.
Just as there were many who were astonished at him —
so marred was his appearance, beyond human semblance,
and his form beyond that of mortals.

+ + +

Nearing mid-morning on the day of his death, Jesus was still being shifted from Caiaphas to Pilate to Herod and back to Pilate. At 8:10, as they were prodding him up the steps to Pilate's palace, Clarence's wheelchair came to rest on his daughter's porch, his heart not so befuddled as his mind. His son Art had just rung the doorbell and was hurrying down the steps to his car. Betty was shouting as she opened the screen door, "I told you never to bring Dad here without calling the day before! Fred has to go into the shop and I'm going to meet Janice for lunch. What am I supposed to do?" Art hollered back, "Our agreement was that you'd take Dad at least every other weekend and I've not heard from you for three weeks!" Soon Betty was on the sidewalk and they were screaming at each other across the roof of the car.

Clarence was staring into some unseen distance, his face showing no sign of emotion or comprehension.

Now Betty was yelling something about their father's will and how Art would have that house free and clear before long. Art was gesturing toward his father saying, "Haven't you been wanting to spend more time with your daughter?" Betty turned and shouted to the porch (with no expectation of a real answer either), "Sure, well I bet you'd rather come when we can plan a nice day like we did after Christmas. Right, Dad?"

She'd already looked away to continue the argument, when they both were startled to hear a loud noise from the porch. Clarence had slammed his cane against the railing. "Dad! Dad? You dare to call me 'Dad'? I'm your father, yes, but you're not acting like my children!"

Art and Betty were dumbfounded. That was the most he'd spoken in weeks. They rushed to the porch. Neither could say a word.

So shall he startle many nations;
kings shall shut their mouths because of him;
for that which had not been told them they shall see,
and that which they had not heard they shall contemplate.
Who has believed what we have heard?
And to whom has the arm of the Lord been revealed?

+ + +

Late in the morning on the day of Jesus' death, he was held in the custody of cruel and taunting soldiers. At 10:35, as Jesus felt a thorny crown placed on his head while he was still reeling from a blow in the back, a young woman named Eloise was walking toward the town market in Coventry. She tried to walk looking straight ahead, but heard the two knights a few paces away laughing at her and felt them making obscene gestures at her as she passed.

Several brothers from the monastery on the hill were coming toward her. As they passed by they buried their faces in their cowls so that they would not have to see her.

She tried to ignore them and think what she needed to buy — some spice, fruit, mutton, and perhaps one of those scarves made in Italy; after all, she had plenty of money.

Then up ahead she saw Lady Anne. Eloise thought she was the most beautiful woman she'd ever seen. Her parents had hoped she'd become one of Lady Anne's attendants. But with her withered arm, the children had always made fun of her. Then when Harold's cousin had come for the archery contest and coaxed her into the stable, she was so glad to be in someone's embrace. The pregnancy was a disgrace. She could never have served Lady Anne after that. Once the baby was born it was easy to be with men at night. And she finally had money to throw in people's disapproving faces.

Suddenly she realized she was trapped and couldn't escape as Lady Anne's attendants came her way. They were giggling. Her face burned and her heart was breaking, though she tried hard not to show it as the girls curtsied to her and scattered rose petals in her path. They doubled over with laughter.

He grew up before them like a young plant,
and like a root out of dry ground;
he had no form or majesty that we should look at him,
nothing in his appearance that we should desire him.
He was despised and rejected by others;
a man of suffering and acquainted with infirmity;
and as one from whom others hide their faces, he was despised,
and we held him of no account.

+ + +

Soon after, on the day of his death, Pilate again put Jesus before the people in the streets. At 11:10, as they shouted "Crucify him! Crucify Him!" a tear ran down Tommy's cheek, looking on from the back seat of his parents' car.

He was watching his classmates' parents demonstrating in front of the school. Some were carrying signs they'd made. One said, "No AIDS or No School." His dad was arguing with Andy's father. Tommy was trying to get a glimpse of his mom.

He still didn't really understand all this about being sick. He didn't actually feel all that bad. But the doctor had said he was very sick. And his parents had told him it was true. It was hard for them to talk to him about it; they were trying not to cry.

Now people didn't want him to go to school anymore. They said he'd make the other kids sick. They'd die. He didn't want anyone to die. Especially his family. But they still hugged him and kissed him, and just said they needed to be careful about some things. He was being very careful.

They'd told him he was going to die. It still scared him a lot. But he was learning to think of it sometimes now without being completely frightened. His parents said they'd miss him but he would still be with God who could take care of him and love him forever. And his pastor was spending time just with him and talking about Jesus' death and being raised from the dead.

There was his mom. She was just saying over and over again, to no one in particular, "What would you do if it were your son? What would you do!" Someone was shouting, "Why do you have the boy here? It only makes him feel worse. It makes it worse for everyone. Get him out of here. Take him away!"

Tommy tried to look past the crowd and see the playground and the baseball field. It seemed a long while since he could play like that. Then, by grace, his mind and his eyes shifted focus, with hope, to something far beyond.

Surely he has borne our infirmities and carried our diseases;
yet we accounted him stricken, struck down by God and afflicted.
But he was wounded for our transgressions, crushed for our iniquities;
upon him was the punishment that made us whole,
and by his bruises we are healed.

+ + +

It was not yet noon when the soldiers laid the crossbeam on Jesus' shoulders and led him through the streets of Jerusalem. At 11:40, as Jesus stumbled, Jedidiah was hoisting two bales of cotton on his shoulders and starting again toward the boat at the levee.

He staggered under the weight and fell to his knees. He rose as quickly as he could, not wanting the field boss to see. He was working for three this morning. Henry was still weak from a whipping, and Isaac had gotten drunk last night and couldn't be roused for work. The master had said as long as their work got done, they would not be sold. The master had almost taken them to Charleston last month.

Jedidiah didn't know how long he could spare them. Isaac was married to his Emma's sister, and Henry and his woman were always so good to them. Emma begged him to do whatever he could for the sake of her sister and their friends and the children.

So he labored on. He didn't dare speak a word of protest. He was singing almost silently under his breath, over and over, "And he never said a mumblin' word. Never said a mumblin' word." The path from the wagons to the levee was a hard one, and the life of a slave was a way of sorrows.

> *All we like sheep have gone astray;*
> *we have all turned to our own way,*
> *and the Lord has laid on him the iniquity of us all.*
> *He was oppressed and he was afflicted,*
> *yet he did not open his mouth;*
> *like a lamb that is led to the slaughter,*
> *and like a sheep that before its shearers is silent,*
> *so he did not open his mouth.*

+ + +

The sun was high over Calvary as the soldiers held Jesus' hands and feet against the cross. Exactly at noon, as a soldier struck the first nail, young Kwe-helo cried in pain as one of the stakes went completely through his right leg and left him dangling upside down.

He cried after his friends, but they had all fled for fear. They had been in search of firewood on the south Kalahari. All of them were playing and running when he had fallen headlong through the thatched grass into a lion trap. His friends couldn't reach him and feared they would fall in too. They surely would bring help.

The pain was excruciating. He had never felt such pain. But he was also brave and did not cry out. Still, he did not know why it should have happened to him. Had he not pleased God? Was he not ready to become a man in the spring?

He could see the branches of a tree overhead. The limbs shimmered in the noonday sun, and as he had lost much blood already, the tree began to swim in the sky.

Sinking into unconsciousness, he prayed his father would come and save him.

> *By a perversion of justice he was taken away.*
> *Who could have imagined his future?*
> *For he was cut off from the land of the living,*
> *stricken for the transgression of my people.*
> *They made his grave with the wicked*
> *and his tomb with the rich,*
> *although he had done no violence,*
> *and there was no deceit in his mouth.*

+ + +

In the early afternoon, Jesus drifted in and out of consciousness on the cross. At 1:50, as Jesus tried to ask for something to drink with lips parched dry, Chung Ni Lin was attempting to raise his head from the sand.

He had lost all track of time, there in the barren vastness of the Gobi desert. All he could think about was finding something to drink. But didn't know which way to turn.

Over a year ago a detachment from one of the main armies of Ghengis Khan had thundered into his village on their ponies. They had taken anything of value, along with most of the food supplies. He realized that it must have been a terrible winter for his family and his people.

The Mongols had threatened to burn his village to the ground unless someone who knew the way would lead them over the mountains and to the great Yangtze River. He had agreed, and in order to save his people, he had left everything he loved.

Now on their way across the Gobi, his captors had abandoned him in the desert to die of thirst and exposure. He longed for his family, his home, for China.

He reached for a sand spider; it would hold a drop of moisture.

Yet it was the will of the Lord to crush him with pain.
When you make his life an offering for sin,
he shall see his offspring, and shall prolong his days;
through him the will of the Lord shall prosper.
Out of his anguish he shall see light;
he shall find satisfaction through his knowledge.

☩ ☩ ☩

In the mid-afternoon, Jesus regained a hazy consciousness for a moment, and murmured a prayer commending his spirit to God. At 3:00, as he breathed out a long, quiet breath and did not again draw breath, Anders the Silversmith was rubbing his eyes; he'd thought he could see his wife running to meet him as he came up the path to their cottage.

But he knew he was delirious. He had not been out of bed for three days. That's when he had fallen so deathly sick. The Black Death, people called it. The plague. Many in the port town had already died.

He'd left home almost a month ago to meet a ship coming into Bergen to buy supplies. Many of the ship's crew had already fallen sick or died. Then it spread through the town. His brother's entire family became ill and now all but his niece had died. More than anything he wanted to go home. But he'd seen how the plague had claimed his brother's whole family. He feared that if he went home his dear Friede and little Nels would die too. He'd written notes to explain why he had not returned home, but he wondered who would live to give them to her.

He heard the thumping of the wheels of the death wagon in the street. The cart went through the town each morning to gather the dead. A man with his face wrapped in rags leaned into the house. Anders lifted his head and tried to speak; he would have told him to send word to Friede. But no words would come.

The man simply called back to the street, "This one's not dead yet." Anders discovered he could not raise his head again. His strength was gone. He prayed for Friede and Nels. He prayed for himself. His eyes closed. They would not open again.

The righteous one, my servant, shall make many righteous,
and he shall bear their iniquities.
Therefore I will alot him a portion with the great,
and he shall divide the spoil with the strong;
because he poured himself out to death,
and was numbered with the transgressors;
Yet he bore the sins of many,
and made intercession for the transgressors.

+ + +

It was dusk. Joseph and the others had taken Jesus' body from the cross and now laid it in the tomb. At 8:12*, just as they were leaving the garden and slowly returning home, a pastor is saying to the congregation, "It was dusk. Joseph and the others had taken Jesus' body from the cross and now laid it in the tomb. At 8:12*, just as they were leaving the garden and slowly returning home, a pastor is saying to the congregation ..." this: that Christ suffered for the world, that Christ suffered *with* the world. Christ still suffers for the world, and he has never ceased suffering with the world. On Good Friday, above all nights, this must be said.

Your hearts hold the joys and sorrows of your whole lifetime. And more than that, through love and compassion, you feel something of the suffering and the hope of the world and of the ages.

In Christ we know that suffering is not a sign of God's absence nor in itself evidence of his judgment. On the cross Christ opened his arms to share the weight of the world's pain: disease and disasters, injustice and poverty, wars and a thousand personal pains even in the most ordinary of lifetimes.

But more than merely sharing the world's suffering, our Lord redeems it through the power of the love of God. As we remember that our Lord died that day, so this day the lights are going out in our service of shadows. Already we look forward to celebrating the resurrection.

In his dying pain he took upon himself our sins. This is our Lord, the suffering servant long prophesied by Isaiah. And by his injury and death, we are healed.

We pray this night our profound thanksgiving for the salvation wrought on the cross. And in knowing Christ shares our suffering and the suffering of the world, we seek strength, courage, healing, and finally, one day, the grace to commend for eternity our lives and spirits to God.

―――――――――

*Use the time on your watch.

Easter Day
Acts 10:34-43

All The World Is Waiting For The Sunrise

Is it tomorrow, or is it still yesterday? In the cartoon, Dennis the Menace is tugging at his dad's covers, and Mr. Mitchell is trying to lift one eyelid. Dennis wants to know, "Is it tomorrow yet? Or is it still yesterday?"

It's a profound question. Something like that — some 2000-year-old Aramaic version of it anyway — must have been in the minds of the women on their way to the tomb. In fact, they went to the tomb fully expecting to find yesterday, and instead found tomorrow. They went expecting death and loss, and instead found wonder and hope.

What if their lives had stayed stuck in yesterday? Life lived just waiting for some tomorrow. Life lived stuck in the meanwhile of waiting.

Once I wandered up into the rooms of the biology department, upstairs from my literature classes. There in a round room of one of the gothic towers, I noticed all these cabinets with narrow long drawers. The musty air was sliced by the afternoon sunlight slanting down from high, narrow windows. I thought I recognized the name on a series of drawers — "lepidoptera" — and opened one. There in shallow boxes in neat rows were dozens or hundreds of butterflies, each suspended on a pin with a fading slip giving its Latin name.

I remember that haunting feeling well, seeing all those transfixed butterflies. All of them just stuck there forever, fading along with their labels. People get stuck too. Maybe they could be labeled right where they're immobilized: "Sandy — Waiting for a New Career Opportunity to Magically Appear," or, "Lee — Still Hoping for a Perfect Romance." What if we're just stuck in yesterday?

"My soul waits," says the Psalmist, "and in his word do I hope. My soul is waiting for the Lord more than those who watch for the morning; more than those, I say, watching for the morning" (Psalm 130). For the morning we wait, for the sunrise. The whole world waits.

In Herb Gardner's *The Goodbye People*, Arthur admits he's always late for trains, sunrises, appointments, people. He feels he's even late for his own life, "... like I left a wake up call for 30 and ... slept right through it. Something terrific was supposed to have happened by now — some reason for shaving and buying shoes and keeping the clocks wound." At his birthday party he suddenly realizes he has really missed something important. "I couldn't remember what I meant to do with it ... my, you know, life."

What about you? Are you stuck in the waiting? In the meanwhile? Stuck in the hoping, the wondering, maybe even working hard, but waiting for something terrific to happen? All Lent we spoke of ways to take stock of our lives, and realized our need for God's grace, our need to make a new beginning. We give thanks that God's grace is present with us to enable us to grow and change. But now, we need to make sure that happens. The danger is that we'll analyze and plan and reanalyze and never get on with it. The danger is we'll never really live, that we expect life must be somewhere up ahead, something terrific, we hope. Until then we drive to work and cook suppers and pay the bills and flip through the channels on TV and do it all again. In this meanwhile, we never really make significant commitments, we never act upon our deepest problems, we never take on the greatest challenges. We're not really living, just waiting to live.

What are you waiting for? What would it take in order to get on with things, to really get down to business? To turn 18? To get married? To get a job you really like? To move into your dream house? To really fall in love — for the first time, or all over again? To put the kids through college? To retire? Along the way years pass, people and opportunities come and go. And we wait.

My mother has always been musical. In any group — from her high school class to the parishes where my father served — people were always aware of my mother's talents in composing and playing the piano. So it could really raise eyebrows when my sister or I would say in a group of people, "Want to hear Dad play the piano?" As people looked on with surprise, Dad would sit on the piano bench where they'd never seen him before and ask, "What would you like me to play?" We'd hesitate, then suggest, "How about 'All The World Is Waiting For The Sunrise?' " He'd say, "Okay. I like that one," and to everyone's amazement, proceed to play it with great flourish. Then he'd wink at us. What people didn't realize was that it was the only tune that Dad knew. When he quit his piano lessons in his youth, he was determined to keep the ability to play just one song. And that was it — "All The World Is Waiting For The Sunrise."

It's a good Easter Sunday title. Deep in our hearts, it is one tune we all know — waiting, longing, yearning for the sunrise, the dawning in our lives.

Easter holds God's response. The dawn has come. The Son has risen. We're not stuck in yesterday. All the promise of tomorrow has broken into our lives.

We have God's love, power and grace to fully live in *this* moment. And the next. And the one after that. We have grace to let go of the hold of a painful past, to change familiar but self-destructive patterns in our lives, to see our lives as truly worthy of joy and purpose. It's not easy to let go of the past until you can take hold of the future. Easter brings that future to us.

The disciples were prepared to live in cherished yesterday. They would have remembered their teacher's words, and when they saw one another they would have recalled old times and recounted the dear and favorite stories with laughter and poignancy and tears.

They'd have honored his memory and made visits to his grave in Joseph's garden over the years. They'd have wanted to keep in touch and vowed to get together more often each time they saw each other. They would likely have lived as better people because of their years with such a great rabbi. They'd have had greater courage in the face of adversity, would have been more kind, just, and faithful. Time would have healed the sorrow of these last days' horror and injustice and death.

But it would have been just an influence in the direction of their lives. Back at the boats on Galilee, life would have returned to pretty much what it had been before. And, in the end, Peter and Mary Magdalene and all the rest would have faced death with all the ancient ambiguities, uncertainties and fears. The world would have gone on the same.

But here's Peter preaching in Caesarea. "We are witnesses," he declared, "who ate and drank with him after he rose from the dead!" He had arrived at the tomb expecting to find yesterday and see the dead body. Instead he found tomorrow; the future had broken into their world. The lives of Peter and the others would never, ever, be the same again. Nor would the world ever be the same.

Here's Peter telling the Gentiles that God shows no partiality and that this gospel is for all. Whoever believes in this Jesus Christ receives forgiveness of sins. And that is the dawn of a new life.

The world waits for the sunrise. And Easter is God's answer that a new day is already come. This is worthy of our most joyous celebration this most holy and happy day.

They say that when the slaves in Jamaica knew they were to be set free on a certain day, they spent all night getting ready. While it was yet dark they began moving by twos and threes out of their huts into village lanes, joined by others coming from the forests and the plains. They streamed toward the highest hill, climbing through the darkness and crowding together at the top, waiting for the day. As the first strands of dawn began to show on the horizon, a ripple of laughter spread through the crowd like a murmur of waves. Then a shout went up and they began to sing in their distinctive rhythm, at last lifting up their hands into the sky at the rising of the sun and crying, "Free! Free! Free!"

However your life has been, don't let it be unchanged by this amazing gospel. Let your wary or weary heart take in the freedom of this powerful story. This story, Peter promises the people of Caesarea and the people in this place, this story has the power to enable us to break free from all that would entomb us — all the bonds, the limitations, the yesterday pain. And this gospel — by God's grace — gives us the courage to venture out to meet our Lord in our own life's tomorrow — a tomorrow which is not fully here but is real, visible, already broken onto our horizon. Now we venture into the life we most profoundly longed for, not the life we've settled for. Not the keeping on that passes for life, but rather the life for which we have hungered and hoped, the life God intended for us.

All this is possible because we know that God has the power to bring life from death. Such an event should be no less wondrous just because we have heard the story so many times. Still, let's try translating the story into a new image.

Christ was netted and trapped by the lies and deceit of cruel men and the weak faith and failed courage of others. His arms were spread wide and pinned to a cross for death. Over his head a label in Latin read "King of the Jews." After death he was shut in the darkness, the stone rolled across the entrance, the drawer closed tight.

Imagine that on the third day, in that musty, empty room there's a faint noise. Then in Joseph's cabinet there's the sound of breaking glass, a box lid shattered. One of the drawers bursts open and a butterfly emerges to perch on the edge. He remains there to move his stiff wings, marks of the pins still visible. After a long pause, he flutters to the top of the cabinet, then around the room and through the window. Across the meadows he spreads the good news. He has emerged not from a cocoon but from the grave! And, in time, he climbs one of those shafts of light all the way to the sun.

The Lord is risen! We needn't be stuck in yesterday. Today it is already tomorrow. All the world is waiting for the sunrise. The Son is risen indeed!

Easter 2
Acts 2:14a, 22-32

Caught In The Acts

"I saw the Lord always before me,"
David said, "you have made known to me
the ways of life."

The Gift Of Wisdom

It's a miracle that you're here this morning! I suspect, though, that what I mean is not the first thing that came to your mind. I sense someone thinking, "The first Sunday after Easter! You bet it's a miracle. They don't call this Low Sunday for nothing!" Someone else is thinking, "Any morning I get up after a busy week and can still get the kids going and fed and dressed and to church, I've accomplished a miracle!" Or "You bet it's a miracle I'm here. I'd fully intended to go play ball, but my Dad made me come here first!" I don't mean that kind of miracle, though I admit I don't underestimate the value of your presence here this first Sunday after Easter Day!

I mean the miracle that began long ago or not so long ago (we're all different ages, and at different stages of our faith's journey), but likely sometime before last Sunday when first we heard the compelling word of God's abiding and gracious love for us. Out of all life's distractions and pain, all the serious and silly reasons to be petty or greedy or bitter or self-righteous or self-important, our hearts were opened to hear and welcome the witness that God was in Christ reconciling the world to himself and that this Jesus Christ is our living Lord. Such miracles, we know, began happening a long time ago.

On another mid-morning, as the sun streamed into the streets of another teeming city, Peter raised his hands and his voice and told the crowds that the disciples were not drunk, but that they were filled with the exuberance of the Spirit of God, and that though Jesus died on the cross, these disciples still served a living Lord!

The narrow streets were filled with busy and idle people. Everyone had a reason to drift by or hurry past. Cheesemakers were setting up shop. Peddlers were plying their wares. Women were going to market. Children were chasing puppies in the streets.

But many stopped and listened. And by the power of the Holy Spirit through the witness of the apostles, their hearts were opened to a life-giving wisdom. This was not just a new way to make cheese, a new sales technique, a new dinner recipe or a new game.

The world, after all, is full of such information. Do you want to remodel your kitchen, or learn about the moon, or grow bigger tomatoes or play the flute? There are libraries and bookstores and seminars and schools for almost everything you want to know.

Almost everything. Except perhaps to know that you're still a valuable person when you're laid off from your job, when your spouse walks out of your life, when the kids make fun of you at school or when you first truly confront the reality of your own death.

Except perhaps to know that there's a real freedom beyond the emptiness of having enough money to buy whatever you want, a real purpose beyond getting and having more, a real sense of wealth in knowing that all we have belongs to God.

Where does one discover such wisdom? Oh, there are books on this, too. Some more substantial than others. But none are so profound as the one which says at its heart, "For God so loved the world that he gave his only Son, that whoever believes in him may not perish but have everlasting life." Peter says, "This

Jesus God raised up, and of that we are all witnesses." Here is wisdom for the joys and challenges we all share, for the sufferings and fears common to us all, for the highest hopes we all hold in our hearts.

Then Peter quotes David, who said that the Lord showed him the ways of life. This was David's testimony, the greatest and most beloved of all their kings, still so dearly remembered in Peter's day across twice as many centuries as since Columbus set foot in the Americas 'til now. Even then, Peter reminded them, David's tomb was still with them. To this day, too, if the present site is to be accepted. For many centuries, David's tomb has been revered to be a vault in a modest little room with peeling plaster and with tables and shelves painted and chipped over and over again. The vault is separated from the rest of the room by iron bars and on it is laid heavy ornate cloth; above it are silver crowns and golden lamps.

Elsewhere in the city the tomb of Jesus is visited as well. Amid brusque priests, cheap souvenirs and a garish and gaudy shrine, pilgrims also visit Jesus' grave within the Church of the Holy Sepulchre.

But the graves are visited for entirely opposite reasons. The tomb of David is visited for what it holds. The tomb of Jesus is visited for what it doesn't hold, for what it couldn't hold. "God raised him up, having loosed the pangs of death, because it was not possible for him to be held by it," preached Peter.

To this gospel he and the other apostles are witnesses. And people stopped to listen. We have heard it too. We, by faith, believe the witnesses. "Blessed are you," Jesus says to Thomas called the Twin. Whose twin? The Bible never tells us. Or maybe it does. "Blessed are those also," promises Jesus, all those who have every reason to doubt and to forget and to clutter their lives with many things, "Blessed also are those who have not seen and yet believe." Who is Thomas' twin? You are. And I.

Yet by grace we may also be made wise, fools that we are. This is not a wisdom we achieve, but a wisdom we are given. We may bear the scars of the disappointments and betrayals and failures of our years, but faith that has triumphed over such challenges is greater witness still.

What do you see when you look at your hands? We all see something different. I count several scars on mine. There's the scar from a fall on the playground when I was very small; a long scar from a slip of the hacksaw when I sawed a lock from my rabbit hutch; a semi-circled scar from an accident with a coke bottle as my sister and I were gathering bottles for the 2 cent deposits; a jagged scar I got cleaning up a spill in the glass aisle when I worked at the A & P. Look over your own hands. Perhaps you, too, have an assortment of scars. What injuries do you still see there?

We all wear scars. Most of them we don't wear on our hands. But sometimes they are visible in the expressions on our faces, the look in our eyes, the firmness of our handshakes or the lightness of our gaits. Sometimes they don't seem to be visible at all, at least not to strangers. But those who know us well see our scars as we cope and strive and dream. The faith that lives beneath those scars is powerful testimony to the resurrection. So it was that first Sunday after Easter when Thomas saw the nailprints in Jesus' hands and fell on his knees before his living Lord.

As through Lent we sought to make a pilgrimage toward wholeness and renewal, so this Easter we will celebrate this new life in Christ. Throughout the ages, Easter Eve was a time for baptism and renewal of baptismal promises. In many of our churches that tradition continues in the Easter Vigil, and if there is not always a midnight baptism, at least there is often a gathering around the font and a renewal of the promises made at our baptism and a celebration of God's promises made to us.

One Order for Baptism includes a prayer for the baptized asking the gifts of the spirit as named by the prophet Isaiah. Often these are named again in the laying on of hands at an affirmation of baptism in the Rite of Confirmation. For the baptized we pray, "wisdom and understanding, counsel and might, knowledge and the fear of the Lord, and joy in the presence of God" (Isaiah 11).

These gifts will form our theme for the Sundays of the Easter season as we hear the witness of Peter and Stephen and Paul in Luke's book of the Acts of the Apostles.

By grace may God teach us the ways of life, and even more, the Way of Life who is our resurrected Lord. May the gifts of our new life be so abundant in us that we may triumph through both the sorrows and the joys of our years, even beneath our scars.

And may we be witnesses too, in our own ways and in our own time, as we too are caught in the Acts, the Acts of the Apostles — the acts of those who belong to a living Lord.

Easter 3
Acts 2:14a, 36-41

Standing And Understanding With The Apostles

Peter, standing with the eleven, raised his voice and addressed them, ...
"God has made him both Lord and Christ, this Jesus whom you crucified."
They were cut to the heart...

The Gift Of Understanding

The word for "stand" in the language of signing is to place your index and third fingers upright on your palm, held flat, as if standing. When I first learned some signing years ago, the father of a deaf boy in my parish was amused to point out that even signing has its slang. There's a proper sign for "understanding," which derives its origin from the learning process it describes. But he noted that there is also a slang equivalent. You take the sign for stand, and turn it upside down.

How very appropriate that sign is for the Spirit's gift of understanding! This spiritual understanding defies gravity and reason; the conventional way of thinking is turned upside down.

So Peter's words to the crowd, which he knows includes many who called for Jesus' crucifixion, are not words of revenge or anger or bitterness. He proclaims to them that God still holds out to them the promise of the gift of the Holy Spirit — "to you and to your children and to all that are far off, everyone whom the Lord our God calls to him." The scripture tells that many were cut to the heart and wanted to know what they could do. "Repent," Peter replies, "turn your lives around." And thousands were baptized, and shared with the apostles in prayer and study and fellowship and communal meals.

We too have heard the good news of the Resurrection. We have been baptized into the life of Christ and the love of God. And now we seek to live — to think, speak, act, hope — as people whose faith is a dynamic power in our lives. Faith is not an accomplishment. It's not insurance that our troubles are over. It's not a lifesaver we put away in case we ever need it.

Our faith identifies us as people who in the turbulence of life are constantly being forgiven, healed, challenged, and called to serve. One of the gifts promised us as we strive to live by faith is understanding.

Among the alternative marriage vows suggested in a liturgical supplement is one which includes these words: "Together we will try to better understand ourselves, the world, and God." Such a vow is certainly worthy of a Christian community as well: "Together, as a congregation, we will try to better understand ourselves, the world, and God."

How do we come to understand ourselves? From our earliest explorations of independence, to our adolescent identity struggles, to our venturing out on our own, to mid-life crises, to the physical and spiritual challenges of our later years, our lives are full of the struggle to understand ourselves.

Why do we do what we do, say what we say, and think what we think? Theories and explanations abound. Some of them are quite helpful. But for a Christian, our understanding of ourselves begins with our baptism and knowing that we are children of God. "What shall we do?" cried the people to Peter. "Repent and be baptized," he exhorted them. The people had an opportunity to begin to understand their own hearts — how they had called for Jesus' crucifixion and now cried for salvation through Jesus.

There are a thousand ways to evade accountability or excuse the sinfulness of our life's brokenness. Not much is going to change unless we acknowledge and take seriously the darkness in our own hearts, and the readiness of God to forgive and empower us.

One sense of understanding in the Bible is to describe the most profound depth of our being, the place where values are formed and issues are decided. We see the maturing of Peter's understanding of himself more than that of any other apostle. We learn of his impetuous sinking in a moonlit lake, his harsh rebuke when he tried to steer his Lord on an easier course, the depth of his failure and pain reflected in his master's eyes by firelight. This same Peter now aggressively preaches to thousands on the streets of Jerusalem, and with the eleven gives witness to his faith.

Our pews are full of such Peters, and Peters in progress. When we seek to deepen our understanding of our concerns and troubles, we don't seek out those who seem to live their lives with ease. Rather, we seek out those who have sunk and survived, or were rebuked and reconciled, or who doubted or denied and now proclaim with their lips and their lives the love of God. Through the experience, compassion and deepened faith of such persons, the Holy Spirit enriches our spiritual understanding.

At best, we will only ever partially understand ourselves, Paul said, as if we could only see ourselves dimly in a mirror.

We seek also to understand the world. It is important, surely, to know what we can of the world. Each of us will only grasp a little of its vast nature. Still, learning languages, studying history and the sciences, discovering other cultures, traveling, keeping abreast of world news — all these are important ways to begin to understand the world.

And yet what we need to understand most is that "God so loved" — not just us — but "the *world*, that he gave his Son." Such an awareness that the whole world is the object of God's affection will rescue us from self-centered and self-serving ways of thought and action.

And how do we understand God? This is the field of theology and the quest of peoples since the beginnings of human history. The studies and writings of theologians all across the history of the church have enriched and challenged our thoughts about God.

But for all we understand, it's important to acknowledge all we can never understand. Luther wrote of the God who is revealed and the God who is hidden. We will always only ever know that fraction of the reality of God which he reveals to us. Thanks be to God that he has shown himself to us in Jesus Christ! In Christ we know him as a God of love, who desires holiness, justice, mercy and peace for his world.

The ways and purposes of God will always be beyond our full understanding. There will always be mystery and a need to accept our inability to understand. This is most painfully true in our times of anguish, when we like Job are left admitting that we who missed seeing the stars first splashed across the sky and singing to their Creator, may not be able to grasp all things. We will work from what we know: that God is a God of love who wills good for us. Whatever is inconsistent with that we reject, even as we seek to live with the questions that remain.

There has always been a place for theological inquiry, and we will want to continue to question and struggle and seek to deepen our understanding of God. But in striving for what we don't understand, we dare never lose hold of what we know best: the love of God in Christ Jesus our Lord.

The two disciples who had walked with Jesus on the road to Emmaus remembered how their hearts burned within them as Jesus had opened to them the scriptures. Some of our understanding comes through words — scripture, stories, hymns, liturgy and conversation. But some of our understanding comes through no words at all, just as the disciples, upon reaching Emmaus, recognized Jesus in the breaking of bread. Some of our understanding, too, comes apart from language — the sacraments, a gentle touch, tears of regret or joy, an affirming smile, a moment of beauty.

The gift of understanding is the ability to see the truth beneath the appearance of things. As on that day when Peter preached, so on this day in Easter, we proclaim that Christ is not dead but alive, not in the past but here among us.

This will be more than enough, until the day when we see God face to face, that day when we will know fully, even as all along, we have by God been fully known.

Easter 4
Acts 2:42-47

Not Independence, But Freedom

All who believed were together...
attending the temple together and
breaking bread in their homes...

The Gift Of Counsel

In a brochure about an AIDS hospice, one of the residents who had recently died was quoted as having said, "The hardest thing about having AIDS is asking for help, but this house is nice for that sort of thing."

A dying man's childlike affirmation of a place to seek and receive help describes one of the deepest needs we bring to our lives in the church. Like the AIDS victim, we've always found that asking for help is difficult. We want to be independent, to stand on our own, to not be indebted to anyone.

But life humbles us. Chance and change across the years force us to realize we're not nearly self-sufficient. None of us has all the answers, resources, or discernment to live a life as fulfilling and faithful as the life for which we pray.

One of the gifts of the Spirit promised at our baptism is the gift of counsel. The only true counsel, for the Christian, is the counsel of God. Now that we seek to live a new life, where do we turn for help? We pray, we study the scriptures, and we live in the company of the people of God.

Our goal, which we held before us all through Lent, was to prepare ourselves to accept the power of Easter and resurrection. But unlike it is with so many goals, our aim was not to go it alone. Do you remember learning to swim? How uncertain and fearful it felt to be surrounded by water? We needed reassurance and someone to hold onto as we learned to breathe, relax, and use our arms and legs to move us through the water. We needed someone there to catch us until we could trust our own ability to stay afloat. With practice, we learned to swim alone, without help from anyone. So it is with so many tasks and skills we've gathered.

Not so, however, with our lives in Christ. Our goal is not to become self-sufficient. I wish I could recall who said, "God did not promise to make us independent. He promised to make us free."

The description of the early church in our lesson from Acts indicates how very much they needed one another and how fully their lives were intertwined. Luke tells that those who believed together also worshipped together daily, ate communal meals, and even held in common all their possessions and income to share as any had need.

That's a pretty idyllic picture! The history of the church ever after is littered with well-intentioned but failed attempts of ardent believers to live in such communities. Unfortunately, or fortunately, much of the rest of the book of Acts shows a more realistic side of life in the early church, and it surely was not a time without conflict. One commentary states, "We misuse Luke's account of Pentecost when we make believe that it offers us a documentary film of the beginnings of Christian mission..."[1] Surely, though, there is truth in Luke's description, as well as hope. The early church was a growing, but small community. They did rely heavily on one another for guidance, assistance, and support. They were learning — and teaching — what it means to be the Body of Christ.

Into such a community we have been baptized. We are made members of a community in which the sins of the world are all too evident — pride, greed, suspicion, jealousy, and all the rest of it. Yet that doesn't fully describe this community, not by a long shot. This is a community which gathers around the gospel of the love of God in Christ our Lord. We learn that love as we hear the scriptures. We receive that love in the sacraments. We also experience that love as we care for one another, and for the world around us.

In seeking to live a new life we must be part of such a community. Where will we turn for reassurance when our confidence falters, or for guidance when we face a new and difficult challenge, or for forgiveness when we have failed ourselves and God?

It's not that we'll ever lack for advice. There's a magazine devoted to virtually every interest you can imagine. The section of self-help books is probably the fastest growing section in the bookstore. Certainly there's no end to the number of people ready to tell us what we should feel, what we did wrong, what we should do next. There are the late night television programs in which half-hour advertisements are dressed to look like talk shows; a panel of experts tell us how to invest our money or lose weight or find a new career. There's always something to buy. Advice from so many quarters has its price.

We can surely get good advice outside the church. If you want to replace your kitchen sink, you obviously can't be sure that someone from church, or any Christian for that matter, will be able to give you better advice than someone else. Nor will a Christian necessarily give you better piano lessons.

But what about advice in dealing with your difficult teenager? Or how about support for dealing with a drinking problem or gambling addiction? Or all sorts of critical and routine concerns? There too, we can't say that those outside the church will give counsel or support less valuable than that from our Christian community. And, in fact, as many of us know, we can receive some pretty unhelpful counsel even from those in the church.

However, in matters that touch such issues as justice, peace, or mercy, only the church, for all its faults, holds itself accountable to the gospel. The church alone holds Christ as its only authority, its only final reference point. So we struggle together to understand what the scriptures teach us relevant to a particular issue. We inquire of the history of the church, of its teachings, what direction to take.

In certain great issues the Church continues to struggle. With some — like peace and war, and economic justice — the church has wrestled through its whole history. New issues continually present themselves. There are biomedical questions now which had never before been considered. But the church is the community where we work to ask the difficult questions, to struggle with complex and even conflicting values, to seek to know the mind of Christ and to have the courage to act upon that wisdom.

For such a purpose, God has bestowed on his church the gift of counsel. It's one of the names our Lord gives to the promised Spirit who will give life to the church — Counselor. Above all the other voices speaking to us, the church strains to hear the voice of one who calls us by name, who gathers us into this community of believers, whose voice we know and trust — the voice of the Shepherd.

This is the community into which we have been baptized, among whom we are called to live, with whom we are sent to serve. Imperfect, to be sure. But always accountable to the love of God in Jesus Christ our Lord. We need one another. Our gospel describes the church gathered together as a flock with one Shepherd. Our lesson describes the intimately intertwined lives of the community of the early church.

We too need one another — to worship and work together, to pray and study and learn and serve and fellowship together.

May God increase in his Church, and in each of us, his gift of counsel. After all, God didn't promise to make us independent, he promised to make us free!

---

1. Ernst Haenchen, *The Acts Of The Apostles*, (Philadelphia: Westminster Press, 1971), p. 189.

Easter 5
Acts 7:55-60

Our Defense In A Stone-littered World

While they were stoning Stephen, he prayed,
"Lord Jesus, receive my spirit... do not hold this sin against them."
When he had said this, he died.

The Gift Of Might

"Jesus loves me, this I know, for the Bible tells me so. Little ones to him belong. They are weak, but he is strong." The children will sing their hearts out, joining in this beloved song. But stand in the midst of a bunch of young children and ask, "Who here is weak?" You'll be barraged with denials, protests, and muscle flexings. The bravado of children is difficult to exaggerate.

An image endures for me. Once a group of young boys from an inner city congregation was spending the weekend in my rural parish, as an aspect of our partnership. As we walked along the canal towpath, each boy boasted more boldly of just what he would do should a bear or mountain lion appear from the woods. (Whether or not they knew that neither lion nor bear had been seen within many miles of there for over 150 years, I wasn't sure.) In the very midst of their claims of fearlessness and daring, a large blacksnake crossed the towpath. You know, of course, what happened next.

It took some doing to round them up again; you wouldn't think they could run that fast. I'm not making fun of them. Children everywhere do precisely the same thing.

It's a sobering and humbling aspect of the maturing process that we begin to grasp and admit our limitations. Not that we're ever free of all pretense to being powerful or wise. But it changes shape and shifts into a variety of subtleties as we grow older.

Indeed, all our lives we admire people who appear to be strong. At nine that may be the tough little kid who challenges his classmates on the playground. At 17 it could be the guy who has a hot car and breaks all the girls' hearts. At 25 it might be the aggressive young executive already climbing her way up the corporate ladder. But at some point, earlier or later, hopefully we begin to see an inner strength, and appreciate its superiority. Might, the promised gift of the Spirit, is that inner strength and the courage to act upon our convictions.

Jews who believed in Jesus as the Messiah still comprised the earliest Christian community as Luke describes it in Acts. But among them were Greek-speaking Jews, and there were complaints that their needs were being neglected. So the disciples chose seven from that group to serve as their designated assistants.

One of those seven was a man named Stephen. All we know of Stephen is Luke's description that he was a man "full of grace and power" and that he did "great wonders and signs among the people." And we know the incident that leads up to today's lesson: how the Jews challenged his preaching, had him arrested and placed before the council where he preached passionately and eloquently. They only became more deeply enraged, and dragged him out of the city and stoned him to death. According at least to Luke's account, this then was the first Christian martyr.

What had Stephen expected? The seven had been chosen to assist in the distribution of food to the widows. They were to wait on tables in order to free the apostles to devote themselves to prayer and to serving the word. To this end they received the laying on of hands from the twelve. Stephen's gifts were broader than that. So he preached. And his preaching was powerful enough not only to encourage believers but to threaten enemies.

Had Stephen heard how Jesus had reassured his disciples the night before his own death? "Don't let your hearts be troubled. Believe in God, believe also in me...Peace I leave with you...not as the world gives. Do not let your hearts be troubled, neither let them be afraid."

Haven't we all wondered how we would fare should we be called upon to lay down our lives for our faith? Haven't you tried to imagine what you would have said given a choice between renouncing your faith and facing lions in the coliseum? Or whether you'd have proclaimed your faith before the sword of the invading Turks? Or if you were threatened with being burned at the stake by the inquisitors? Or awaking to a contingent of secret police bursting into your home in the night? Christians, we know, have died in all these and countless other circumstances. And surely across the ages the blood of the martyrs has challenged and inspired the Church.

Stirring hymns call us to follow their example. Many of us first learned Reginald Heber's hymn in our youth, calling us to follow the example of Stephen and the twelve.

> *The martyr first, whose eagle eye / Could pierce*
>   *beyond the grave,*
> *Who saw his master in the sky / And called on him to*
>   *save.*
> *Like him, with pardon on his tongue / In midst of*
>   *mortal pain,*
> *He prayed for those who did the wrong / Who follows*
>   *in his train?*
>
> *A glorious band, the chosen few, / On whom the Spirit*
>   *came,*
> *Twelve valient saints; their hope they knew / And*
>   *mocked the cross and flame.*
> *They met the tyrant's brandished steel, / The lion's*
>   *gory mane;*
> *They bowed their necks the death to feel / Who*
>   *follows in their train?*
>
> (from "The Son Of God Goes Forth To War")

Our modern world has had its martyrs as well. Some are celebrated and remembered by millions: courageous witnesses to the truth and the gospel such as Pastor Dietrich Bonhoeffer, Dr. Martin Luther King, Jr. and Archbishop Oscar Romero. Others, of course, have died for the faith the world over, to be remembered by many or a few. Could you follow in their train?

Few of us will ever know. But that surely doesn't mean we don't need the gift of might, courage and strength. I heard a prominent Catholic theologian say once that though one dare never devalue the witness of the martyrs who did in one moment spill out their life's blood for the faith, one dare not devalue either those whose blood flows moment by moment, hour by day, year after year in service of the gospel.

This is the call to most of us: to live the faith with courage and integrity and might in the very unspectacular places where we live and go to school and work and swim and shop. Here we need the might to give witness to our faith in the most ordinary of circumstances. The gift of might then can take many forms: to befriend the unpopular kid in class, to refuse to join in a racist joke in the lunchroom, to be faithful in a relationship even when we're discouraged, to live more simply and give more charitably when we could afford more for ourselves. In these and countless situations every day we have opportunity to show the courage and might which is ours by the grace of God.

To live with such might is to live full in the faith. To deny and desert our faith is to fill our life with little deaths — deaths of our hope, and our spirit, and peace. Sometimes our fears are real and sometimes they are exaggerated. In the cartoon strip *B.C.* the consistently cowardly knight Rodney rushes in to see the king. "The whole army is in disarray and in flight. We saw the Huns approaching but never thought they would attack." "Why," asked the king, "did you think they'd not attack?" Rodney nervously replies, "Because there were only two of them." ("Cowards die a thousand deaths...")

The opposition, however, is usually all too real. And sometimes to do the unpopular but faithful thing wins others to our side but often it does not. We need to be able to see that in these commonplace daily situations our faith is in a life and death struggle.

Such invisible realities are expressed in more startling language in ancient times and by primitive peoples. A story in the *Baltimore Sun* about such a primitive tribe deep in the Lacondon Forest on the border of Mexico and Guatemala quoted one of the elders regarding such a truth. The old man observed that long ago his people had behaved properly in the homes of the gods. He told how everyone said — and knew it was true — that a person who would desecrate the homes of the gods by breaking a stone would die. "But now," the old man lamented, "our young people break the stones and shout, 'It is not true! See! I break the stones in the house of the gods and I do not die.' But they do not see that every time they break a stone, they die!"

We die too each time we deny our Lord, whether we realize it or not. In so many familiar places, in routine situations, with people we know well, we have an opportunity to give witness to the love of God. Or, we deny, betray, make excuses, fail; then our faith is shaken and we die inside. None of us is fully, consistently faithful. So constantly we seek forgiveness, reconciliation and renewed life.

The challenges to our faith will never be few. In the Holy Land, one can't help but notice how the ground is littered with stones. The enemies of Stephen and the gospel would have had no trouble finding ammunition to attack him. All they had to do was reach down. The enemies of the gospel around us have no more difficult an effort.

God increase in each of us the gift of his holy might.

Easter 6
Acts 17:22-31

Paring Down Our Pantheons

Paul stood before the Areopagus and said,
"Athenians, I see how extremely religious you are in every way...
What therefore you worship as unknown, this I proclaim to you."

The Gifts Of Knowledge And
The Fear Of The Lord

"Tell me a story," said the little boy to his dad at bedtime, "tell me a story and put me in it." There are no stories to which children pay better attention than those in which they play a part. Even as the years go by, and the eager child becomes one of those cool, disinterested teenagers, watch how she perks up when you say, "I remember the time that you...."

Adults will follow the same pattern. At an annual congregational meeting, suppose we show a series of slides of the Holy Land; some of you surely will be interested. But the next year, suppose we show slides taken at congregational events all year long. Won't everyone be looking with rapt attention, searching in the pictures for themselves and those they know best?

Paul shows the same savvy with the people of Athens. He doesn't begin by saying, "I have a gospel to proclaim to you that is so different from this impersonal pantheon of gods and goddesses that it will knock your sandals off!" No, he begins by having found a niche in their own story. They had one altar dedicated to an unknown god, just to make sure they had it all covered. Paul takes this admission of uncertainty, this possibility of another god they'd not yet discovered and announces, "I'm going to tell you about this God, whom you do not know, but I do know." In the end, the nature of this God would topple all the others from their columns, tear down all their altars. But that's not how Paul begins.

The Greek world was one of active intellectual inquiry. They made remarkable advances in science, mathematics and other fields. Paul was pressing their theology. It's not enough to simply muse about what exists. It is critical to decide what you do about it, how you live.

Charles Krauthammer told a story in a commencement address, to urge graduates to move from knowledge to action. There once was a sultan who awoke troubled in the middle of the night and summoned his wizard. What unraveled his sleep, he exclaimed to the wizard, was the mystery of what is holding up the earth. "Majesty," assured the wizard, "the earth rests on the back of a giant elephant." The wizard's reply pleased the sultan and he lay back to sleep. But then, drenched in a cold sweat, his sleep was interrupted again, and again he summoned his wizard. "What's holding up the elephant?" he demanded of the sleepy wizard. The wizard looked him in the eye and said, "The elephant stands on the back of a giant turtle." Wearily he started back to his bed, when he suddenly turned around saying, "And you can stop right there, Majesty. It's turtles all the way down!" Krauthammer made sure they got the point, warning them, "My friends, don't get lost in the study of turtles."

Paul had something to say to the Athenians about what held up the earth, and who created it. But he was anxious to move them beyond study and discussion into transforming their lives.

For Paul, knowledge of God is not a matter of idle speculation, as it was discussed in much Greek philosophy. To know God is to have an active, dynamic relationship with him. To know God is more than to recognize him. It is to serve him, obey him, praise him, love him. In Hebrew, for a man to "know" a woman, as frequently stated in the Old Testament, is to have sexual intercourse. This is not a euphemism to spare a more graphic description; rather, it conveys the extremely intimate and personal knowledge a man and woman gain of another through their sexual relationship. To know God is to be engaged in a very personal and profound relationship.

Yet there's another dynamic to this relationship. This is the absolute awe with which a believer stands before God. Scripture calls it fear, but it's not the fear of which we usually speak. It's a profound awareness of the complete holiness and absolute power of God. It's an awe which made Moses hide his face and Isaiah fall to his knees. "This God whom I proclaim," Paul says, "lives in no shrine and needs nothing we could give him. He has created everything in its place." Before him, the Athenians should repent, because though he is the Creator "indeed he is not far from each of us."

How easy it is to be fearful of things at hand, rather than to be in fear — awe — of that which has genuine and ultimate power over us. I recall hearing of an incident that took place during the battle of Antietam during the Civil War. Union soldiers were crossing a farm to attack the Confederate battle line drawn in a sunken road thereafter called Bloody Lane. The Confederate fire was deadly and Yankees were falling in increasing number. As the Yanks were passing the farmhouse, some of the Confederate bullets struck the Roulette's beehives. Soldiers recalled how in the midst of deadly gunfire they were running in circles trying desperately to avoid the angry swarms of bees. How easy it is to fear a minor but pesky danger rather than a greater, less immediate one. Moving the stakes up a notch, Jesus once said, "Don't fear those who can kill the body but not the soul. Rather fear him who can kill both body and soul in hell." Then he went on to say, "Don't be afraid; he watches over sparrows. You are of more value than many sparrows."

This is the paradox Luther cites over and over in his explanation of the Ten Commandments. Again and again he says, "We should so fear and love God..." Our fear and our knowledge, our love and our awe are all bound together. We don't have the blessing, or curse, of dismissing God as irrelevant because he is so distant, nor imagining our relationship as so chummy that we have him in our pockets. We can't hate him for dangling our salvation just tantalizingly and frustratingly out of reach, nor assume the love of God makes him a doting grandparent who can't say no, even for our good. Each possible heresy is held in check by the paradox of the other. We receive the gifts of both the knowledge of God and the fear of God. How then, do we use such gifts?

We learn that the truest thread through all the events and relationships of our lives is that which is lived within the story of God's love for us. Our awe of God keeps us respectful of the jealousy of our God, and our knowledge of our God enables us to trust in his grace.

Such a God surely deserves our full loyalty, undivided praise, and complete obedience. What foolish people were those Athenians to have a whole pantheon of gods! We still know their names — Zeus, Hera, Kronos, Aphrodite and the rest. The gods all had their own spheres of influence, their particular interests, their own points of contact with human lives. It seems ridiculous. We'd never worship a whole pantheon of gods! Would we?

Do you suppose a teenager ever says to himself, "I'd like to invite Donna to the Spring Dance, but the other guys don't think she's very pretty, she doesn't dress really great... but she's really pleasant. Maybe she's not a knockout, but then I know I'm not either. They'd make fun. I don't know. Maybe I'll just stay home." What makes a guy pass up a chance at an enjoyable evening, even the possibility of a longer relationship? Call it What-Everybody-Else-Thinks-Is-More-Important-Than-What-I-Know-Is-Right. Put it on a column. It's a start.

After hearing the announcements at church Sandra squeezes her bulletin hard, and whispers to her husband under her breath, "All this money for world hunger just when we're getting ready for vacation. We gave some money at Christmas. Who knows where it all goes anyway? I'm not going to feel guilty just because we want everything that's best for our family." Let's look for another column. And let's put on it, Me-and-Mine.

It's not difficult to see how we could go on to list many

things, values and ideas which compete for God's sovereignty over our lives. "A god," says Luther, "is that to which we look for all good and where we resort for help in every time of need; to have a god simply means to have something in which the heart puts all trust." So we obviously have many gods, competing in different ways, at different times with our loyalty to the God whom we know in Jesus Christ.

It's not that we want to ignore God. He's there too. He's in charge of Sunday mornings, weddings and funerals, babies being born and life after death. But that's not enough for our God. He demands it all. Our God will not for one millisecond remain content in a pantheon.

I understand, and the scriptures certainly indicate that God does too, how difficult it is to remain completely loyal, entirely obedient. It's not an easy thing for a teen to diverge from the consensus of his friends. It's easiest to talk about peer pressures among youth, but at any age we are pulled toward certain patterns of thought and action which are more typical of a group of people with whom we associate. We like to fit in, to be well thought of, to meet people's approval. Sometimes even if it means we risk what we know, by faith, is right.

It's easy, too, to frown disapprovingly at someone holding out on an appeal for the hungry. But none of us have given all we have to the poor. How much is enough? Who of us doesn't have many more luxuries than we need? Who of us isn't aware of what seems to be an endless need for food and help? We all wrestle with the challenge of sacrifice and responsibility.

All of our lives we'll be struggling to know what is the right choice, what is the faithful course, what is the loving thing to do. Indispensable gifts are the knowledge and the fear of God, as we live in awe of his holy and selfless jealousy, and trust in his boundless love.

Easter 7
Acts 1:6-14

People With A Mission

"You will be my witnesses in Jerusalem, in all Judea and Samaria, and to the ends of the earth."

The Gift Of Joy In The Presence Of God

"What I have here is really going to turn things around in this country," he said. "Maybe even the world." Actually, he didn't have very much to say. He just kept eating, trying not to seem famished, and all the while never letting a bulging, tattered briefcase off his lap.

It wasn't the Sunday noon dinner I had pleasantly anticipated. But there had been a knock on the front door just after noon. Though I'd long before taken down the brass plaque identifying my home as the Lutheran parsonage, I had a feeling that my grandmother was right: hobos do have charitable homes secretly marked — especially on Main Street in a small town. Here stood a man in a crumpled blue suit, wearing a tie giving evidence of his menu over the previous several weeks. He was carrying an old suitcase and clutching a briefcase close against his chest.

So we ate our lunch together, this hungry man, this man with a mission and I. Where had he come from? "Everywhere," he said.

"I've been everywhere." Where was he headed? Everyplace, who knew where it would take him? Then he pointedly added, "Right now I'm on my way to Washington." He had little else to say. His mind seemed distracted by his mission. And the food. He didn't even say goodbye as he trudged up the hill with his suitcase.

Usually we have but one contact with such a person, but several years later I saw him hitchhiking on a major highway, miles away. I might not have recognized his face, but the clutched briefcase was unmistakable. Was I going his way? I said I was, just for a chance to hear more of his mission.

I reminded him of our lunch years earlier and he nodded, but with the muddled recognition of someone who'd eaten thousands of lunches in kitchens across the country. I asked about his trip to Washington. He didn't answer. But perhaps he did sense that this was our second meeting and he could divulge something of his purpose. He patted his briefcase. "Colors," he said, "everything has to do with colors. You already have the whole spectrum. Look around, colors are everywhere you turn. You just have to make them work for you." Before he got out he patted his briefcase again, eyes wide and said, "It's going to change everything. It's going to change the whole world." Watching him in the rear view mirror as I drove away I was moved by the pathos of his appearance and circumstances, but also by his devotion to his mission. Clearly he did not share the same mental reality with the rest of the world, but for several years he had clung to his cause, or some changing cause. Yet it seemed all the more pathetic because whatever was in his briefcase was not likely to change the world; it may not even have changed him.

How different the purpose that propelled the disciples! They too had a mission. "You are my witnesses," Jesus had told them at his ascension, "in Jerusalem, in all Judea and Samaria, and to the ends of the earth." They would never be the same. The whole world would never be the same again.

This is our calling, too, our baptismal vocation. "Let your light so shine before others that they may see your good works and glorify your Father in heaven." So we have prayed for the increase in us of the gifts of the Spirit. The last of those named by Isaiah and included in a baptismal liturgy is the gift of joy in the presence of God.

Many of us learned to sing at camp, "I've got that joy, joy, joy, joy down in my heart..." Unfortunately too many Christians have that joy so far down in their hearts that no one can see it! That surely was not God's intention.

Easter had not begun with any easy, giddy joy. In fact, Matthew reports that the women ran from the tomb "with fear and great joy." Mark says the women fled seized by "terror and amazement" and that they were afraid. How did they come to know such joy?

Had they been afraid that Easter dawn only because they realized they were in the presence of the most holy God who wields the power of life and death? Or perhaps they now realized how faithless they had been, how little they had understood. What would God do with them now? What might they expect should they see the Lord, now risen from the dead?

Whatever the cause, Jesus overcomes their fear. He appears among them bringing peace. He walks with them on a country lane and breaks bread with them at their table. He makes a fire on the beach and invites them to a breakfast of bread and fish. In his presence they are forgiven, empowered, challenged, loved. John would later write, "We declare to you...what we have heard, what we have seen with our eyes, what we have touched with our hands...so that you may have fellowship with us...so that our joy may be complete." This is their mission as they are now witnesses, "my witnesses," Jesus says, "to the ends of the earth."

What mission are we pursuing? What do we guard as dearly as my dinner guest with his briefcase? As pathetic as he may appear, there are many today whose purpose in life is not much more fulfilling, or meaningful, or faithful.

What real, ultimate difference does it make to spend so much energy to indulge ourselves even more than we have, or to seek such relentless revenge on someone or some group for real or imagined injuries we feel we've experienced? What does it matter that we strive for power at all cost in some territory of life we've staked out? What about any of those petty, shallow, empty reasons that motivate so many people to press on day after day?

For his disciples, Jesus had prayed, "Holy Father, protect them...that they may be one, as we are one...I speak these things in the world so that they may have my joy made complete in themselves." There's far too much energy to increase the world's pain, ugliness, brokenness, envy, self-fascination, violence, prejudice and greed. But by grace we can increase the good, the kindness, the beauty, the peace, the mercy, the generosity and love in the world. We can increase the joy.

Joy as God promises joy is not a momentary distraction from life's troubles. It's knowing that we can entrust our troubles to God for his healing and help. Joy from God is not delight in another's loss as if it were our gain. It's knowing that we are precious to God and that the gains and losses of others do not diminish or enhance our value. God-given joy is not a way to focus on the present to avoid worrying about the future. It's the knowledge that the future belongs to God and nothing will separate us from his love for us in Jesus Christ, not even death.

There's a place for the laughter of children and our pleasure with friends. There's need for appreciation in the lovely and terrible beauty of the changing seasons. There's profound hunger for the affirmation of being loved. And there's joy in all these experiences and more.

But the greatest joy the world can know is that promised by the angel over the shepherds' field near Bethlehem: "I bring you news of great joy for all the people. To you is born this day a Savior."

To this we too are witnesses. The promise of joy is for our life now. But not only now. The need for joy before the approaching of death may seem very far away to most of us. (But not all of us.) Time passes. Time was when our years were but a handful and each year stretched on for what seemed forever from birthday to birthday. The time will come — for some of us it has come already — when our arms are full and overflowing with years which seem to pass like one of those long-ago summer days, when we burst into the morning sunlight one moment and the very next moment it seemed we were being tucked into our prayers.

For that time, in the gathering dusk of your own life's day, don't underestimate the contentment of knowing that the gift of joy in the presence of God is not only for this world, this time alone.

Until then, the Lord charges, "You are my witnesses." Until then, may the joy of God increase in our hearts, and its overflowing be a powerful witness for the gospel.

Ascension Of The Lord
Acts 1:1-11

Sometimes Goodbye Is Hello

Goodbye, even with someone you deeply care about, isn't always sad. At least it isn't only sad. Sometimes it can be like saying hello.

Some of us have said goodbye to children. We bundled them up and coaxed their little eyes and hands to say "bye bye." Soon we waved them off to the neighbor's and school and camp. And at some point along the way we said goodbye to our children for the last time. And we miss our little boys and girls. But we know that had we not done so, we'd never have had the joy of greeting the men and women who share the world with us in a whole new way and go on to invent their own lives.

Sometimes you say goodbye to a friend for the last time. Months or years of meeting and parting, of greetings and leavings gone, you find you've said goodbye to this friendship forever. And you welcome the beginning of a new relationship. Still friends, but now husband and wife. And one goodbye makes possible a new hello.

To gain by losing. To hold fast by letting go. To become something new by ceasing to be what we were before. These are truths at the heart of the gospel. And nowhere is this clearer than in the story of Christ's ascension.

Our Lord spoke to the disciples often about his certain leaving of them. But, as it is for all of us when we are happy, they treasured his presence so much they couldn't imagine his departure. It was one of the last and most difficult lessons they learned.

"Where I am going you cannot come." And, "a little while and you will see me. Then a little while and you will not see me." And "I am going to prepare a place for you." But if they had any hopes of his being with them always as it had been, it was shattered one Thursday evening and Friday noon. And they knew it could never be the same again.

It wasn't. That's clear even in all the testimony about the risen Christ among them. It's the same, and yet not the same. He appears and disappears. They don't recognize him and then they do. And this doesn't last either.

After a time, he departs from them, not ever again to be with them in the same, recognizable way. From Luke, we have this handling of the transition from the way things were after the resurrection, to the way things are as you and I experience it: that the Risen Christ is no longer bodily with them to laugh and eat and teach, but has returned to divine glory. "Up" was the only way he could describe it. So we call it the ascension.

It's hard not to think of up. But maybe it's more like moving up to the fourth grade, or to vice-president, or just growing up. Then the early church struggled with what was next. Jesus had spoken often of coming again. So they waited. But years and generations passed. The wrestling with this issue crowds many of the pages of early Christian writings, including some of those in the Bible.

Finally, it dawned on the Church that the divine presence for which they were waiting was already with them. They had inherited Christ's mission, and with his ascension into glory, his power was in them. With this realization, all the waiting for the second coming became at best a secondary concern. Having said goodbye to Christ before them and beside them, they were able to greet the Christ who lived within the body of the Church, within them.

We sometimes still wish he were with us, as he was then. I loved the song I learned in Sunday School that expressed my fond yearning, as I listened to all the Bible stories of the days "... when Jesus was here among men, how he called the little children like lambs to his fold; I should like to have been with him then." That's an understandable but childish side of our faith. We learn to be grateful that he's with us now.

Our lives are full of so many letting go's and beginning again's that the ascension is a good story to ponder often. Each letting go of ages and places in our lives has its sting. And how much more the loss of loved ones. Whenever we lose someone we love, there's an emptiness in our hearts, a yearning that will last as long as we live. We know by faith that time will pass and healing will come but the pain until then is all too real.

So God sends his Holy Spirit, and we cling to his church. God comforts us for present and past pain, gives hope for the future and guidance along the way. And there's meaning in our waiting as God enables us to share our pain with others, and enables them to share their pain with us. Our longings have the taste of salvation. Our sorrow can be channeled into sincere prayers and gracious acts.

Outside the body of Christ we would be alone, in isolation and despair. Questions like "Can I be a Christian without going to church?" lose all relevancy when we discover that the fullness of our lives depends on this Body of Christ.

So Christ had ordered the disciples to remain gathered in Jerusalem to wait for the promise of the Father. They were to receive power when the Holy Spirit would come upon them and ever after be witnesses to the love of God in Christ Jesus, even to the ends of the earth. Even here, even now. We are his witnesses and he is with us still.

One day every loss will be counted as gain. Everlasting life will be the ultimate rebirth. And until then we will spend our days with the people of God.

Our lives have been changed, transformed. There's no going back. I can remember my grandmother with a mixing bowl at her kitchen table, stirring a wonderful combination of ingredients for a cake or cookies. Dad and his brothers would tease her, because she insisted on always stirring in the same direction. All logic and evidence to the contrary, it just seemed to her that if you stirred backwards, it just might all become undone.

But it can't be undone. Not the batter in the bowl, nor the web of relationships and events, grace and goodness, sin and fear, sorrow and joy which make up our lives. This journey we've begun again — of repentance, reflection, and renewal, of the gifts of God's grace to live a new life — this can't be undone. We can depart from it, we can fail to continue, we can deny it — but we can't go back to being the people we were before we heard again this amazing gospel. Our world is not the same; it never has been since that Christmas, Good Friday, Easter, and Ascension.

By faith we see that all these weeks and years of our lives, all these ordinary moments, are, in reality, filled with extraordinary grace.

From 3.8 billion miles in space, the earth is merely a blue dot in an ocean of black. That was the observation of scientists several years ago as they looked at a photo taken from deep space near the edge of our solar system. The astronomer Carl Sagan further observed, "On that blue dot, that's where everyone you know, everyone you ever heard of, every human being who ever lived, lived out their life."

But the disciples staring into space 2000 years ago already knew that isn't completely true. From the infinite and divine realm, God had entered the world in Jesus Christ. Across several years the disciples had walked with him the dusty roads of Galilee. Now they had experienced the leaving of their Lord. And yet he was still with them. They had said goodbye. But to say goodbye was also to say hello.

And what is it, really, to say "Good-bye"? Once, centuries ago, English-speaking Christians parted saying, "God be with ye." In time, it became "God be wi' ye," and finally, "Good-b'ye." Jesus' ascension fills the phrase with the full power of its meaning. In his ascension "Good-bye" truly means "God is with you." When the voice of Jesus says "Good-bye," we hear "I am always with you, even to the close of the age."

Books In This Cycle A Series

Gospel Set

God In Flesh Made Manifest
Sermons For Advent, Christmas And Epiphany
Mark Radecke

Whispering The Lyrics
Sermons For Lent And Easter
Thomas Long

Christ Our Sure Foundation
Sermons For Pentecost (First Third)
Marc Kolden

Good News For The Hard Of Hearing
Sermons For Pentecost (Middle Third)
Roger G. Talbott

Invitations To The Light
Sermons For Pentecost (Last Third)
Phyllis Faaborg Wolkenhauer

First Lesson Set

Hope Beneath The Surface
Sermons For Advent, Christmas And Epiphany
Paul E. Robinson

Caught In The Acts
Sermons For Lent And Easter
Ed Whetstone

Tenders Of The Sacred Fire
Sermons For Pentecost (First Third)
Robert Cueni

What Do You Say To A Burning Bush?
Sermons For Pentecost (Middle Third)
Steven E. Burt

Veiled Glimpses Of God's Glory
Sermons For Pentecost (Last Third)
Robert S. Crilley

Second Lesson Set

Empowered By The Light
Sermons For Advent, Christmas And Epiphany
Richard A. Hasler

Ambassadors Of Hope
Sermons For Lent And Easter
Sandra Hefter Herrmann